Access your online resources

Understanding Dissociative Identity Disorder is accompanied by a number of printable online materials, designed to ensure this resource best supports your professional needs

Activate your online resources:

Go to www.routledge.com/cw/speechmark and click on the cover of this book

Click the 'Sign in or Request Access' button and follow the instructions in order to access the resources

Praise for this Guidebook

Lindsay's wealth of experience, understanding and knowledge in this field – coupled with her gift and passion for educating others – makes this a book not to be missed by anyone with an interest in trauma and DID. Therapists embarking on work with clients in this field will find this a useful tool to add to their kit. Those with DID, along with their partners and friends will find this both reassuring, hopeful and wonderfully informative.

Jennifer & Parts

An encyclopaedic gift to clinicians; an empowering tribute to survivors and a generous guidebook to all those who love and support them. This essential guide offers a rich tapestry of information, traversing trauma's challenging landscape in a narrative that is relational, accessible, and expansive. It is instructive, illuminatory, and exploratory, a testament to humankind's capacity for courage and resilience in the face of depravity and heinousness. We applaud the author in her phenomenal achievement of disentangling the complex web of dissociative disorders and thank her for her dedication to the field.

Michele & Parts

Well done to Lindsay Schofield for providing such a thoughtful, rigorous overview of key aspects of diagnosis, treatment and everyday life and aspirations. It provides a substantial companionship to the Picture Book but is also valid in its own right. Her tone is respectful and deshaming and helpful for survivors, survivor-professionals and clinical teams.

Dr Valerie Sinason, *Poet, writer and retired child psychotherapist and adult psychoanalyst. Founder Patron of the Clinic for Dissociative Studies and President of the Institute for Psychotherapy and Disability; 2016 Lifetime Achievement Award ISSTD*

This guidebook around DID and its companion picture book provide a rare insightful and yet accessible set of resources. They should go a long way towards demystifying DID, addressing some of the common misconceptions, and offering hope and support to those impacted, as well as those walking alongside them.

Dr Cathy Kezelman AM, *President Blue Knot Foundation – National Centre of Excellence for Complex Trauma; lived experience survivor*

Wow, this book is awesome! Very impressive. Lindsay has condensed the current knowledge in this field into a comprehensive and clear guide for people who are seeking to heal from trauma of all kinds. What a phenomenal resource!

Dr Lynette Danylchuk, *Past President ISSTD, 2019 Lifetime Achievement Award ISSTD*

This wonderful book presents trauma science in a thorough and thoughtful way that is accessible to survivors, practitioners and allies. Lindsay imbues this resource with clinical wisdom and compassion that will empower survivors to understand complex trauma and dissociation, and guide both survivors and practitioners towards the goals of wellbeing and safety.

Dr Michael Salter, *Scientia Associate Professor of Criminology, Postgraduate Coordinator UNSW Australia*

This is a rich, practical, comprehensive and succinct resource gem that combines readable and understandable guidance for clinicians, clients, and their supporters about child & adult dissociation! It is a must read for all who come in contact with those with dissociation!

Frances S. Waters, *Author of Healing the Fractured Child: Diagnosis and Treatment of Youth with Dissociation, Past President of ISSTD, & Chair of ISSTD Faculty Director of Child & Adolescent Psychotherapy Training*

This book, beautifully written by Lindsay Schofield and beautifully illustrated by Cassie Herschel-Shorland, is for people with dissociative disorders, especially DID, and those who are aiming to help and support them. It is easy to read and yet provides in-depth and well-informed information and signposting to more technical material. It won't tell you how to do therapy if you are a therapist, but it will set you on the path. I really like the way it addresses everyone, therapists and clients and families and friends alike, as people interacting with DID and related problems.

The book provides a nice introduction to trauma, its effects and hope for healing, as well as how it leads to dissociation in varying degrees. It provides an overview of assessment, conditions and treatment models. A chapter for survivors is written in accessible language and includes a checklist to use when seeking help from professionals, along with handling flashbacks and grounding. A chapter for practitioners gives advice on tools and self-care. The guidebook moves on to reflect and comment on the sister book "*Our House: Making Sense of Dissociative Disorder*", showing survivors how to use the book and offering more resources.

This book will make a difference in our field, making the mysterious accessible for everyone.

Dr Fiona Kennedy, *Director, GreenWood Mentors Ltd. BA (Hons) M Clin Psych D Clin CPsychol AFBPS CPsychol, Fellow BABCP*

Understanding Dissociative Identity Disorder

This accessible guidebook has been created to be used alongside the picture book, *Our House: Making Sense of Dissociative Identity Disorder*, as a broad introduction to childhood trauma and its legacies, with a focus on dissociation and DID.

This clear and easy-to-read resource offers an insight into trauma, its continuing effects and the continuum of dissociation. Practical exercises and opportunities for reflective discussion are included throughout to encourage personal engagement either individually or through treatment. Written with clinical accuracy, warmth and compassion, it will expand the reader's knowledge of DID and deepen the understanding, application and usefulness of the picture book.

Key features include:

- Photocopiable and downloadable resources and activities designed to develop a richer and more personal understanding of the development of DID
- A page-by-page insight into images from the picture book
- Further reading suggestions and information about treatment and support for survivors, as well as for the family, friends and professionals who journey with them.

Bringing clarity to a complex issue, this is an invaluable resource for survivors of trauma and for those who support them, counsellors, psychologists, social care workers and other professionals, as well as family and friends.

Lindsay Schofield is a Consultant Psychotherapist with a private practice in Surrey, England. She has worked in private practice for two decades, providing treatment and support to individuals and couples, helping them with a wide range of emotional and mental health challenges. A specialist in trauma and dissociation, she has dedicated thousands of hours to learning about and working with survivors of complex trauma. With a strongly relational and collaborative approach, the Picture book and Guidebook set were born out of a desire to make the complex clear and to bridge divides wrought by traumatic experiences and misunderstanding.

Lindsay has written and delivered her own workshops in the UK and internationally, and provides supervision to practitioners working in different contexts, clinical and pastoral. She is accredited with the BABCP, the BACP (Senior), the ACC (Supervisor), the NCS (Senior/Supervisor) and the NCP (Senior). In her spare time, she enjoys a menagerie of animals and nature.

Cassie Herschel-Shorland is a freelance designer, illustrator, and artist. She works predominantly on increasing access to the diverse history of places, objects, and people's associated stories. As an active tutor Cassie is also passionate about supporting mental health and wellbeing through creative workshops often in museums, galleries, or libraries; encouraging people to explore and illustrate their own stories.

Cassie has BA(Hons) in 3D design, post graduate certificate in illustration and a Master of Arts in historical illustration. She is a fellow of the Royal Society of Arts.

Understanding Dissociative Identity Disorder

A Guidebook for Survivors and Practitioners

LINDSAY SCHOFIELD
ILLUSTRATED BY CASSIE HERSCHEL-SHORLAND

Routledge
Taylor & Francis Group

LONDON AND NEW YORK

First published 2022
by Routledge
4 Park Square, Milton Park, Abingdon, Oxon OX14 4RN

and by Routledge
605 Third Avenue, New York, NY 10158

Routledge is an imprint of the Taylor & Francis Group, an informa business

British Library Cataloguing-in-Publication Data
A catalogue record for this book is available from the British Library

Library of Congress Cataloging-in-Publication Data
A catalog record has been requested for this book

ISBN: 978-0-367-70819-1 (pbk)
ISBN: 978-1-003-14812-8 (ebk)

DOI: 10.4324/9781003148128

Typeset in Antitled
by Deanta Global Publishing Services, Chennai, India

Access the companion website: www.routledge.com/cw/speechmark

Dedication

I have great admiration and respect for the courage and honesty of survivors and their parts, especially those known to me, who have dared to trust me, and to allow me to share their journey of recovery.

These things should not have happened – it was not right, and it was not fair.
You are worthy, you are stronger, you are resilient.
I will hold steady for you.

I also offer huge thanks to the outstanding professionals who have led the way in this work – sometimes at cost to themselves personally as well as professionally.
Your daring and integrity is seen and valued.

References and recommendations to works that have informed and inspired this material, and the author's work with clients, are cited throughout, and in Chapter 7: Additional resources.

Contents

Thanks to

Clare, my editor, for encouraging me to extend the scope of these books; for your light touch, responsive and warm professional support – and for sharing a little of Indie! Thanks also to Leah and the team at Speechmark for getting these books into print.

Jennifer & Parts, for proof-reading, insights, quotes, encouragement, and for your trust – "I'm still holding tight".

Michele & Parts, for proof-reading, quotes, and generous feedback – "there will be a path for you".

Sue Richardson, for your ongoing steady support and for stepping up when times were tough; for selflessly giving your time and expertise reading drafts and for offering helpful suggestions.

Valerie Sinason, for your enthusiastic and generous encouragement early in the process. I wrote your comments down, and they sustained me!

David Lane, for your support and affirmation, for connecting me to Routledge, and especially for helping me find Cassie!

Cassie Herschel-Shorland – the most *excellent* of illustrators and people – *thank you*! You took on my brief, embraced my storyboard and drew with such empathy for "our child". Your talent and sensitivity to the project has been a delight, and your flexibility and willingness to make changes has made working together really satisfying and a pleasure. I wish you all the success you deserve!

My family, for your love, enthusiasm, and patience. Projects like this don't happen without a backup team – so for encouragement, technical support, cooking, tea-making and rescuing creatures big and small – special love and thanks to my steadfast husband who keeps me whole!

Introduction

This Guidebook is written as a companion to the picture book, *Our House: Making Sense of Dissociative Identity Disorder.* The metaphor of a life being like a house, presented in the picture book and elaborated in the Reading Deeper chapter in this accompanying Guidebook, developed in my mind through my work with individuals who have experienced either trauma or negative experiences in childhood. However, the ideas presented are not entirely novel, but grounded in therapeutic theories and practice taught by many great clinicians who have gone before me.

Frequently, and for many reasons, individuals struggle to acknowledge childhood experiences of loss or trauma. When difficulties develop through insecure attachment, inadequate provision, or an absence of the conditions they need to prosper, individuals tend to blame themselves for consequent problems. It is difficult to notice what is *not* there, and even harder to discern that your experience is "wrong" when you do not know what "right" looks like or what should be available to you. This doesn't miraculously become clear as we enter adulthood, so without knowing differently, we continue blaming ourselves for difficulties, faults or omissions believing they prove there's something wrong with us; other times, individuals feel the need to protect those responsible for their mistreatment, whether from neglect, insufficiency, or deliberate harm, because of their own beliefs about loyalty or through strong attachment needs. You see, we all need love, security, meaning and purpose, and in the absence of these conditions, we will strive to create them, even if they are only illusory. Our physical, emotional, and psychological survival depends on them, and we will seek to create any sense of those conditions in order to get by. This may be done knowingly or unwittingly, since it is sometimes too painful, frightening, or risky to admit that those who should care for us are inadequate or may even represent the source of our pain.

Dissociation is a word that has been used to describe symptoms of varying severity; it has also been interpreted differently by professionals working in various settings with diverse models. You may be familiar with the phrase "I'd rather be anywhere but here"; when survival or sanity is dependent on not being here, dissociation may develop as a powerful protector. DID and dissociation provide a psychological defense against trauma, against conditions or conflicts that simply "should not be", and protects children and the adults they become from circumstances that cannot be tolerated, stably endured or processed.

There are many excellent treatment guides for therapists, providing rich insights and instruction for working with dissociation. This set does not aim to compete, but to offer an accessible and user-friendly insight into trauma, especially the effects of ongoing traumatic experiences and resulting dissociative difficulties for those diagnosed with DID or dissociation, for their friends and families, and to complement resources available to those helping them.

DOI: 10.4324/9781003148128-1

The largest section of this Guidebook – "Reading Deeper" – provides additional insights into the images and text in the picture book, and how they might be explored and elaborated in treatment either by oneself or with a professional. Please be aware that for simplicity, the picture book presents the development of DID with just one "everyday self" who is present more often and has a greater sense of life across time, and several "parts of self", who emerge to cope with traumatic experiences. However, individuals may have just one everyday self and one part, or they may have numerous everyday "selves" who assume daily responsibilities and roles and many parts.

Finally, to those of you who have experienced trauma, I know that words can enable you, support you and create understanding – or they can leave you feeling undermined, hurt or hindered. My desire is to use words and terms that achieve the former, and yet even amongst those with whom I work, choosing a designation – a title for those with traumatic histories – that satisfies everyone has not been possible. Please bear with me as terms are used interchangeably – "individual", "client", "survivor"; they are used with respect for your courage, your expertise, and hopefully you will hear the language of partnership, equality and respect in these pages.

Trigger warning

Although it is not possible to predict what will be triggering to everyone, I have placed a broken "t" – a trigger symbol, beside potentially challenging sections.

A trigger is something that activates (or "sets off") a reminder of traumatic experiences. It may be something we recall from the event, or something which is linked to the memory but is often outside of conscious awareness. It can provoke reliving of different parts of the memory, images, sensations, thoughts, feelings – or any mix of those things.

It can be disorienting or distressing ... but it is *memory*.

The content of this book has been presented with care, but it is possible that survivors of abuse may find some aspects triggering or challenging. The destabilization caused by triggers is temporary, but it is important to take care of yourself and to avoid any action that would cause you further harm; in fact, to do the opposite of any negative or harmful behavior.

If you are triggered: remind yourself of the current date, of your surroundings, that you are no longer at risk (if you have achieved safety), that you are able to take care of yourself now and that *you are simply remembering old things ...*

1. Calm your body – slow down your breathing, walk in cool air, relax your shoulders.
2. Calm your mind – notice things around you and label them, do a counting exercise or repeat a rhyme to call your mind back to the present.
3. Block unhelpful urges – if you feel like doing something hurtful or risky, respond with a protective or caring action; reach out to a trusted friend or seek an environment that will help you stay okay.
4. Identify what helps and make a prompt card to help remind you when triggers occur.

Be compassionate with yourself – triggers take time to resolve – you are learning and growing as you develop new responses.

1 What is trauma?

Trauma creates injury ...

It shatters and breaks ...

It lingers and erodes when good is withheld from us and our needs are not met...

It breaches our defenses and touches us at our core.

It can leave a raw emotional wound that causes ongoing pain, a psychological scar that numbs feeling and prevents growth, and breaks down healthy boundaries.

It does not care who we are – it overpowers us, it terrifies and makes us feel small.

> At the moment of trauma, the victim is rendered helpless by overwhelming force. When the force is that of nature, we speak of disasters. When the force is that of other human beings, we speak of atrocities. Traumatic events overwhelm the ordinary systems of care that give people a sense of control, connection, and meaning.[1]

When a traumatic *event* occurs, it creates a story of "before", "during" and "after" –

It can make it heart-breaking to remember "who I was".

It can steal "who I was meant to be" – and hide or put out of reach, a meaningful future.

> Trauma "arises from an inescapable stressful event that overwhelms people's coping mechanisms".[2]

When traumatic experiences *continue*, when necessary care or protection remain absent, when we are betrayed by those closest to us, or hurt by those who are meant to care for or protect us – the devastation escalates and steals our sense of self and time;[3] it causes tremors within when care is unpredictable or uncertain and can seem to define "who I am", at the same time as obscuring self-understanding – stripping away joy, safety or connection in daily life.

Trauma is a word desensitised by everyday use. A job interview, a stressful day, or a bad haircut are *not* "traumatic". Trauma produces pain and anguish that threatens who we are, our integrity and our capabilities. It occurs when our ability to respond is overpowered by real or perceived threat and leaves a lasting imprint on our mind and body that undermines our ability to relate to the world, to others or to ourselves.

DOI: 10.4324/9781003148128-2

Trauma is also misunderstood, avoided, denied, and ignored. We do not want to listen to, let alone to believe the stories we hear, because the feelings they elicit seem to threaten our confidence in justice and safety and the illusions we hold dear. The shame from traumatic experiences can damage our sense of self or our confidence in a nonthreatening world; we avoid them to protect our own sensitivities or to escape the feelings of inadequacy they provoke.

When trauma is experienced in childhood, it not only harms the healthy development of a sense of self – an awareness of who we are – but it also harms healthy development of the brain, limiting the integration of memory, our ability to feel at ease inside and our confidence in knowing who we are. It produces inflated levels of stress hormones that cause lifelong damage and harm to the body. Circumstances contribute to its effects and impact, which means that our response to trauma is affected by its nature, as well as by our age and our experience of it; the younger we are, the more likely trauma-related conditions will occur and persist.[4]

Trauma and abuse

It is easy to make the mistake of believing that some forms of abuse are worse than others. In fact, emotional and psychological abuse or neglect can generate the same devastating effects as physical or sexual violence and harm. Present in most forms of abuse, they are a toxic stressor, silently eroding hope, health, and potential.

 Forms of abuse:

✚ Emotional and psychological abuse

⌂ includes criticising, humiliating and shaming, name-calling, blaming or scapegoating, threatening, silencing, shouting, sarcasm, inappropriate exposure to upsetting situations as in witnessing abuse or drug taking, manipulating, bullying, gaslighting, false accusations, controlling, intimidating, or forcing someone to perform degrading acts.

✚ Neglect, which includes:

⌂ physical – failing to provide basic needs of shelter, food or clothing, insufficient supervision and protection, insufficient attention to care and hygiene

⌂ emotional – ignoring, consistently overlooking, being absent, failing to promote wellbeing or development, failing to praise or express positive feelings

⌂ educational – failing to ensure appropriate learning and/or schooling is provided

⌂ medical – failing to provide for health needs.

+ Physical abuse

  ⌂ includes hitting, punching, strangling, shaking, pushing, pulling, grabbing, hair-pulling, throwing things at someone, spitting at someone, burning or scalding, suffocating, making someone swallow something that makes them ill or that hurts.

+ Sexual abuse

  ⌂ includes age-inappropriate exposure to sexualised behaviour, images or messages, sexual behaviour that is non-consensual (including sexual acts with children or vulnerable adults who are not deemed able to give informed consent), coercion to sexual behaviour, unwanted kissing or touching, degrading sexual remarks, producing sexual images or movies of minors, grooming, sex trafficking, forced prostitution, bestiality, necrophilia, sodomy, incest, rape.

+ Spiritual abuse

  ⌂ includes the misuse of religious texts or position to coerce, control or take advantage of another individual, manipulating tenets of faith or their expression to serve one's own interests to the detriment of others; ignoring and minimising another's beliefs, point of view or distress with negative impact on their faith, enacting distorted and depraved spiritual ceremonies.

Trauma – Capital "T" or small "t"

When a terrible event has occurred, when it has been witnessed or when others agree that something dreadful has happened, we are generally able to acknowledge our experience and the traumatic response provoked. Events that are commonly recognised as traumatic by their severity, or by the terror or horror they evoke within us, have been called "capital T traumas".

Lesser understood or recognised are the effects of neglect, and psychological or emotional abuse and harm including bullying, poverty, and community stressors and threats. Despite evidence that their effects can be as profound and as severe as the actions more generally associated with abuse,[5,6] "small t" traumas, described as such because singly they may go unnoticed, be ignored or minimised, have a cumulative effect. They are like a thousand small cuts,[7] producing lingering harm and damage and their impact may be the final blow to a child already struggling to cope.

Some survivors want or need to overlook the significance of these traumas, rather than face the stigma or feel the pain of childhood victimisation, mistreatment or the meaning characterised by such terms. It may feel crucial to dismiss or to ignore such experiences in order to maintain the illusion that "my childhood was normal", "it wasn't that bad" or numerous other beliefs we maintain to protect us from the pain of facing the truth.

When a child's sense of safety or attachment to a safe caregiver is destabilised, their physical, emotional and psychological development is damaged, and their ability to make sense of the world, to figure things out, to engage with learning and to develop good relationships is undermined.[8]

Adverse childhood experiences – ACEs

ACEs are trauma by another name. They were identified following a US study[9] in the 1990s and include serious, stressful, or traumatic experiences, grouped into areas of abuse, neglect and household dysfunction. Experienced directly or indirectly, they produce toxic levels of stress that harm a child's healthy development and cause accelerated aging.[10]

Those identified include:

+ physical, emotional, and sexual abuse

+ physical or emotional neglect

+ experiencing or witnessing violence or abuse inside or outside the home

+ parental separation, including imprisonment of a family member

+ having a close family member attempt or die by suicide

+ household mental health problems or substance abuse

+ homelessness

+ discrimination

+ natural disasters or war.

The effects of ACEs are accumulative. Quite simply, as their number increases, so too does their harmful impact, which includes lifelong problems with health, social abilities, and compromised learning potential. Negative consequences include depression, substance abuse, smoking, heart and liver disease, increased numbers of sexual partners and sexually transmitted diseases, unplanned pregnancies, violent close relationships and suicide attempts.[11]

Adverse Childhood Experiences – ACEs

witnessing

neglect

verbal abuse

sexual   abuse

physical abuse

deprivation

separation

substance abuse

Who is affected by trauma?

64% of us are likely to have experienced one or more categories of ACE.[12]

Any of us can be affected by trauma – and how we respond to it does not mean we are weak or strong, foolish, or clever, bad, or good.[13] In fact, there is evidence that how we deal with trauma may be encoded in our genes and passed through the generations – outside of our choice or control. Those who are already disadvantaged or struggling are more likely to be affected and consequences may persist for a long time.

How we experience trauma differs in relation to our circumstances, our age, our personality, our character and according to the support and care we receive, which can make a significant difference to our recovery. Those who are otherwise "strong" or whose lives have been good but sheltered, may be more profoundly affected by the unexpected; the overwhelm can shatter self-beliefs held by the strong; discovering that the world is sometimes cruel or hostile can steal beliefs that the world is safe or full of promise.

Imagine three individuals witness the same road traffic accident. Although they witness the incident from the same vantage point, our three individuals are different ages, and different heights. What happens to them, and what they see and hear is affected by their age, height, and ability to make sense of what is happening, and by their ability to take care of themselves.

Some may be more affected by features of the incident, by what they see, or by what they hear, some may be disoriented by its speed and seeming chaos, whilst others may see the event happening as if in slow motion. If there is flying shrapnel and they are hit by it, the same pieces of wreckage may cause devastating effects to some, and less harm to others: an adult witness who is struck in the leg by a piece of debris is likely to be less harmed than a child who is struck on the head.

For our three witnesses, this event may be distressing, but with reassurance and appropriate treatment they can recover and gather learning that enables them to restore confidence in their ability to take care of themselves in future. The response and care they receive from important others – including family and friends as well as health workers, is likely to play a key part in their recovery. The absence of necessary care, safety – or *simply being unnoticed*, may equally contribute to their struggle to recover.

When our needs are unnoticed, overlooked, minimised, or ignored, our wellbeing, recovery and self-sufficiency is harmed. Childhood trauma carries a legacy.

What are the effects of trauma?

Different parts of the brain are responsible for different jobs. The "brainstem" controls physical systems and life support, the middle (limbic) brain governs emotional and behavioural regulation and the top (cerebral cortex) part of the brain directs rational thought, learning and language. During a traumatic experience, survival mechanisms activate and provoke automatic responses for protection outside of conscious control. The parts of the brain that are responsible for rationale and reasoning close down as the body mobilises for defence. Some brain areas shut down completely,[14] affecting an individual's ability to make sense of things, or even to express themselves. The imprint of trauma is physical, emotional and psychological.

It is normal to have ongoing difficulties for a while after a traumatic event is over. People report mixed effects and feelings, continuing to feel scared, being on edge or jumpy, not sleeping well, or having bad dreams and memories of the event at unexpected times, feeling sad, angry or guilty – sometimes all at the same time. It is confusing and disorienting.

When negative or frightening experiences repeatedly occur in childhood, the developing brain becomes more sensitive to stress. As a result, the body produces an elevated level of cortisol that impacts its ability to establish healthy functioning, impairing its immune system, changing brain structure and disrupting functions of memory and learning.[15] Prolonged toxic stress affects the parts of the brain that deal with fear, anxiety and impulses, and causes them to remain overactive and hypervigilant, scanning for threat and risk as a default activity. Even when safety becomes achievable, the legacies of traumatic experience can remain, and keep individuals stuck in a survival loop. They are constantly on guard against danger, unable to differentiate cues of safety or threat, emotionally reactive, re-experiencing reminders of trauma in nightmares, flashes of events, waves of emotion and intense fear, struggling to form trusting relationships, often sabotaging the good and deliberately punishing or harming themselves.

> Hypervigilance is exhausting.
> (Jennifer & Parts)

Severe and ongoing experiences of abuse lead to complex presentations of PTSD, significant dissociative difficulties, and fragmentation of personality and self. This is addressed further in the chapter: Dissociation: a continuum.

Chronic and complex trauma[16]

This refers to trauma that is repeated or ongoing. It is often invasive and interpersonal in nature, committed deliberately and secretly on individuals for whom escape is either impossible or hard to achieve. It also occurs when neglect is severe or when emotional and psychological abuse creates hostile and harsh conditions.[17]

Whilst severe experiences such as torture, being a refugee or "trafficked" are forms of complex trauma, it most often begins in childhood or adolescence through abuse or domestic violence[18]. It is most likely abusers will deny it ever took place, placing a further burden of mistreatment on those who endured it.

Shame and power are key features in complex trauma, especially when children are hurt by someone in a position of control, or by someone who is meant to be safe. It is difficult for most people to believe that abuse can be deliberate and sustained. We want to believe that child abuse is rare, so the suggestion that it occurs more often than we want to admit or that it is deliberate and sometimes involves organisation, is hard to face. However, survivors have been forced to live with secrecy, shame, and intimidation, and we can help turn the tide by offering openness, empathy and empowerment. It is time we helped survivors shed the false shame pressed onto them by abusers who told them they "would never be believed", that "they wanted it [the abuse]", that "they would be rejected" or that the abuser would "hurt [someone or a pet]" if they told. The imperative to keep the secret, or even to "not know or remember" is a burden they should never have had to carry. Lifting shame so that survivors can reclaim their dignity, and breaking the silence[19] so they can reclaim their voice and their rights is an imperative in recovery.

 ## When our carers hurt us – *a trauma of betrayal*[20]

When those who are meant to care for us, protect us, support or help us, cause or inflict trauma, the terror and conflict we experience is immense. The unconscious neural and physical bond we have with parents and our main caregivers remains *regardless of the quality of care given.*[21] This attachment comes at a high cost, when children must find ways to excuse and defend those on whom they depend. It is too much for them to face the truth that their world and that those who are meant to protect them are unsafe – perhaps that safety is not even possible. When it is not possible to face the truth, but we know that something is badly wrong, we find ways to blame ourselves in an attempt to take back control of the situation. When a child is powerless to change the adults or their environment, they look for things over which they believe they have control – themselves.

 ## Organised abuse[22]

Organised abuse occurs when one or more abusers collude to abuse one, or a number of related or unrelated children. It can include the production and distribution of sexual images, as well as grooming and prostituting children for a perpetrator or group's gain; it can include darker themes of torture, degradation, and extreme cruelty. Abusers can network in multiple ways, through family, youth or sports clubs, religious or community groups, institutions and via the internet and electronic devices, including computers, mobile phones, and games consoles. They may be motivated by belief, personal gratification, ambition, power, and/or financial gain.

Organised groups are experienced as all-controlling, intimidating, violent, and exploitative and survivors have typically faced discrimination, disbelief, and marginalisation. Chillingly, research indicates that organised abuse is comparatively common[23]. In the clutches of such groups, adult survivors report ongoing sexual assault and victimisation and child protection agencies report recurrent contact with victims.

<<>>

The good news ...

is that science is showing that the effects of trauma can be resolved, and its lasting impact is recoverable.

Trauma and epigenetics

Epi means "on top of", and "genetics" refers to our genes.

Epigenetics is an area of scientific research that helps us understand how our environment, experiences and behaviours affect our genes, their expression, and how those effects influence mind and body.[24]

Our DNA is inherited from our parents, half from our mother and half from our father, and is what makes each of us unique. It contains instructions for growth, development, and reproduction, and can also influence our personality, our character and even our moods.

THE SCIENCE BIT![25]

There are approximately 50 trillion cells in the human body, each containing around 6 linear feet of DNA. Our genes are encoded within our DNA and give each cell the instructions it needs, to know what to do and what to become. During development, positive and negative experiences and environments produce chemicals within our bodies which leave tags, called epigenetic marks, on our DNA.
These marks can change the chemical arrangement of our DNA and affect how the cell "reads" the instructions in the underlying genes, influencing whether or not genes are turned "on" or "off", and how the cell looks and behaves.

Put simply, healthy and unhealthy experiences leave chemical marks on our genetic codes that influence how cells behave, what they look like, and what they do. This begins even before we are born. A mother's experiences and environment, including the food she eats, the stressors she encounters, the vitamins she takes, the alcohol she consumes or the cigarettes she smokes, can transmit chemical signals through her bloodstream to the developing embryo, where they make epigenetic marks on the foetus' own genes and affect its life-long health and wellbeing.

We are affected by nature *and* nurture at the most basic levels of who we are.[26]

However, epigeneticists have also shown that introducing care and nurture can reverse negative effects, even at a biological level, and that healthy functioning can be restored.

In other words, it is never too late to repair many negative effects of trauma, both for ourselves and for its impact on others, including our own children. Our potential may still be reachable and providing tenderness, support and safe conditions for children increases their chances of enjoying a good life and fulfilling their promise. Neuroscience is producing even more good news ...

Neuroplasticity

Neuro refers to nerves and the nervous system; *plasticity* means "reshapeable". Neuroplasticity, also called "brain plasticity", refers to our brain's ability to reorganise itself, to change how it is wired and to create new or different connections.

THE SCIENCE BIT!

When we are born, our brain has more connections than we need, and throughout our lives it removes connections that are not needed. In keeping with the "use it or lose it" rule, or "neurons that fire together, wire together", connections (synapses) that are used often, have strong links, whilst those that are rarely used are deleted.

The brain can change its structure by remapping its neural networks and producing new neurons, making changes at a cellular level. Whenever we learn something new, an action or thought, and repeat it, it is reinforced, and the brain develops and changes. Think for example about how we learn new skills, like learning to ride a bike – we practise, repeat, practise, repeat, and the skill is encoded indefinitely. *With the right mix of stimulation, repetition, and intensity we can change, or "re-wire" the way our brain works.* Our brains can improve our health and performance by making new connections every day and this can continue throughout our lives, regardless of our age or health and helps us to adapt, to learn *and to recover from injury.*

Neuroplasticity not only confirms that recovery from the effects of trauma is possible, but it also elaborates some of the ways in which we can treat its legacies to create growth and lasting change.

Not least ... *kindness*

Kindness is a superpower

Kindness has been shown to boost our immune system, to increase the health of our hearts, to lower blood pressure, to boost self-esteem, to reduce pain, to decrease stress and to improve relationships.

Witnessing or practising acts of kindness causes the brain to release chemicals that contribute to wellbeing and positive mood. Oxytocin is produced, helping us to feel better, and playing an important role in creating bonds of relationship and trust; serotonin can also increase to help regulate mood.

Kindness is protective, nurturing and sustaining, and has been shown to decrease the impact of trauma, both in current time and in lasting effects. Whilst one act of kindness may boost our wellbeing, practise and repetition can help us build a biochemical storehouse for resilience and recovery. It translates into an act, a gesture, a word, or an attitude. It can be given away, but also needs to be given to ourselves.

Notes

1 Herman, J., 2015. *Trauma and recovery*. New York: Basic Books, p. 33.

2 Kolk, B. and Fisler, R., 1995. Dissociation and the fragmentary nature of traumatic memories: Overview and exploratory study. *Journal of Traumatic Stress*, 8(4), pp. 505–525.

3 Danylchuk, L. and Connors, K., 2017. *Treating complex trauma and dissociation*. New York: Routledge/Taylor & Francis Group, p. 8.

4 Hart, O., Nijenhuis, E. and Steele, K., 2006. *The haunted self*. New York: Norton, p. 26.

5 West, M., Adam, K., Spreng, S. and Rose, S., 2001. attachment disorganization and dissociative symptoms in clinically treated adolescents. *The Canadian Journal of Psychiatry*, 46(7), pp. 627–631.

6 Felitti, V., Anda, R., Nordenberg, D., Williamson, D., Spitz, A., Edwards, V., Koss, M. and Marks, J., 1998. Relationship of childhood abuse and household dysfunction to many of the leading causes of death in adults. *American Journal of Preventive Medicine*, 14(4), pp. 245–258; Felitti, V.J., & Anda, R.F., 2011. The relationship of adverse childhood experiences to adult medical disease, psychiatric disorders and sexual behaviour: Implications for healthcare. In Lanius, R.A., Vermetten, E. & Pain, C. (Eds), *The impact of early life trauma on health and disease*. Cambridge: Cambridge University Press, pp. 77–87.

7 "Death by a thousand cuts" refers to a form of torture and execution which was banned in 1905.

8 van der Kolk, B., 2014. *The body keeps the score: Mind, brain and body in the transformation of trauma*. UK: Penguin; see also note 6.

9 See note 6.

10 Colich, N., Rosen, M., Williams, E. and McLaughlin, K., 2020. Biological aging in childhood and adolescence following experiences of threat and deprivation: A systematic review and meta-analysis. *Psychological Bulletin*, 146(9), pp. 721–764.

11 Nadine Burke Harris, 2000. How childhood trauma affects health across a lifetime. Ted.com. Available at: www.ted.com/talks/nadine_burke_harris_how_childhood_trauma_affects_health_across_a_li fetime

12 Working with the World Health Organization, the CDC (Centers for Disease Control and Prevention) provide an infographic on their website: https://vetoviolence.cdc.gov/apps/phl/resource_center_infogr aphic.html (accessed 1/10/20).

13 Dan Siegel, 2019. YouTube, 2021. *Why trauma affects some people more than others*. Available at: www.youtube.com/watch?v=yb4dgkkOkEk (accessed 25/8/20).

14   van der Kolk, B., 2014. *The body keeps the score: Mind, brain and body in the transformation of trauma.* UK: Penguin, Chapter 3: Looking into the brain.

15   Excessive stress disrupts the architecture of the developing brain. Developingchild.harvard.edu. 2021. Available at: http://developingchild.harvard.edu/wp-content/uploads/2005/05/Stress_Disrupts_Architecture_Developing_Brain-1.pdf (accessed 5/2/21).

16   Ford, C. & Courtois, C.A., 2020. *Defining and understanding complex trauma and complex traumatic stress disorders,* in C. Ford & C.A. Courtois (eds), *Treating complex traumatic stress disorders in adults: Scientific foundations and therapeutic models*, 2nd Edn. New York: Guilford Press.

17   West, M., Adam, K., Spreng, S., & Rose. S., 2001. Attachment disorganization and dissociative symptoms in clinically treated adolescents. *The Canadian Journal of Psychiatry*, 46(7), pp. 627–631.

18   Middleton, W., 2013. Ongoing incestuous abuse during adulthood. *Journal of Trauma & Dissociation*, 14(3), pp. 251–272.

19   Middleton, W., Stavropoulos, P., Dorahy, M.J., Kruger, C., Lewis-Fernandez, R., Martinez-Taboas, A., Sar, V. & Brand, B., 2014. Child abuse and the dynamics of silence. *Australian & New Zealand Psychiatry*, 48(6), pp. 581–583.

20   Freyd, J.J. & Birrell, P.J., 2013. *Blind to betrayal: Why we fool ourselves we aren't being fooled.* Hoboken, NJ: John Wiley & Sons.

21   Sullivan, R.M., 2012. The neurobiology of attachment to nurturing and abusive caregivers. *Hastings Law Journal*, 63(6), pp. 1553–1570.

22   www.organisedabuse.com/info

23   See note 14 and Salter, M., 2013. *Organised Sexual Abuse.* Oxford: Routledge.

24   Cary, B., 2018. Can we really inherit Trauma? *New York Times*, December 10, 2018.

25   Griffins, C., 2012. TEDxOU, 2012. Epigenetics and the influence of our genes. Available at: www.youtube.com/watch?v=JTBg6hqeuTg&t=320s (accessed 5/2/21).

26   Yehuda, R. and Lehrner, A., 2018. Intergenerational transmission of trauma effects: Putative role of epigenetic mechanisms. *World Psychiatry*, 17(3), pp. 243–257.

2 Dissociation: a continuum

"I'd rather be anywhere but here ..."
– but what if there is no choice, but to be here?
Here, where your world is overwhelming, painful, terrifying, and constantly so?

Dissociation exists on a continuum – a scale – expressing itself in different ways, with varying complexities and intensities. Some people experience it as a side-effect of drugs or alcohol, or as a symptom of other mental health problems, but it has well-established links with traumatic events.[1] It may occur when overwhelm prevents experiences from being successfully processed and stored,[2] or it may be the ultimate defence when no other protection or escape is achievable.[3] To leave the terror of now, to manage to escape when physical escape is impossible, is the dream of the victimised or the defenceless, the tortured or the powerless. It is a superpower, and the ultimate rescue, when the mind helps us run away from what our body cannot escape. To survive without falling apart, without drawing attention in ways that could cause further devastation – the mind finds relief and safety somehow.

Experiencing dissociation in response to trauma is a normal response and may be life-preserving

Memory is affected by traumatic experience

Memory[4] is dependent on brain development, and both are affected by the conditions and experiences we have as we grow. It is held in the brain and the body, and is dependent on processes of encoding, consolidation, and retrieval.

✛ *Encoding* is the process by which experiences, and sensory information are stored, similar to saving data on a computer

✛ *Consolidation* is the process by which a memory is stabilised, sometimes unconsciously at a biological level, to make it available at a later stage

✛ *Retrieval* refers to the processes involved in remembering and bringing something back into consciousness.

All these processes can be affected by trauma.

When traumatic experience overwhelms or overloads the brain with information, some of its areas shut down to favour responses needed for escape or self-preservation. The information from these unresolved experiences is then held in the body and the brain in disconnected neural networks, as fragments[5] of experience and "split

DOI: 10.4324/9781003148128-3

away" from awareness. When these experiences are provoked into consciousness, they may recur in their original form, but without context, clarity, or sequence; they may "replay" in bodily experiences or sensations, or as visual or emotional flashbacks, causing distress, disorientation, and confusion.

Fragmented memory and amnesia are common symptoms experienced by trauma survivors and in those who have borne witness to traumatic events. They have been observed in relation to all forms of trauma – including accidents, natural disasters, military service, terrorism, medical procedures, and situations involving threat to life – as well as in survivors of assault and childhood abuse.

Types of memory[6]

Memory takes two basic forms, each held in different areas of the brain and the body. Some memory is practical, and facts related, other memory prompts emotion or sensations.

+ *Explicit memory* is divided into two categories: *semantic* which can be deliberately recalled and expressed, and *episodic,* which is autobiographical and includes conscious awareness of experiences and their sequence, general knowledge, and facts.

+ *Implicit memory* is also divided into two categories: *emotional* which connects us to our feelings and needs and reminds us of the feelings we had during experiences, and *procedural*, which includes sensations and movement and helps us remember how to perform tasks, like riding a bike.

Traumatic memory tends to be implicit, which influences its availability and the way in which it returns to mind. It can intrude unexpectedly, as disconnected sensations, feelings, images, or sounds. Without warning and without context, it is akin to an internal assault and its affects cause anguish and suffering. Individuals describe feeling "out of control", or that they are "going crazy". These characteristics have caused some to cast doubt on the reliability of this traumatic memory, but it has been shown to be as accurate as other types of memory[7].

An analogy – "the memory cupboard"[8]

Most memory is a construct of image, sound, place, sensations, thoughts, and feelings. Traumatic memory has been likened to a cupboard into which things were thrown – urgently and haphazardly. Sometimes this might prevent the door from closing on the contents, and other times things might press on the door and fall out. Throwing them back inside may add to the disarray and make it difficult to make sense of the memory. The contents of the cupboard still belong to the memory, but without order and with some aspects difficult to retrieve. Trauma may not be remembered with absolute accuracy, it may be "forgotten"[9] – dissociated – and later recalled, but that does not mean it is unreliable nor untrue.

Memory is particularly related to the disruptions experienced in DID[10], and vital for the construction of self-identity. Fortunately, the elaboration of detailed memory is not essential to healing, nor is it necessary to establish the accuracy of memory to resolve trauma's lasting effects. However, finding ways to accept what has happened, and exploring the meaning of events, are important elements in recovery.

Dissociation

Dissociation is a common symptom of trauma. It causes disconnection and division in personality[11], in memory *and* in physical and emotional experience. A dissociative disorder (DD) is identified when symptoms linger and cause unhelpful disruption to everyday life. Receiving a DD diagnosis does *not* define an individual – but simply describes problematic and disordered functioning in daily life alongside the activation of psychobiological defenses.

Dissociative disorders (DD)[12]

DD exist on a continuum, a scale, and include:

+ *Depersonalisation* – feeling disconnected from your body and your emotions. People report feeling detached from themselves, as if they are watching themselves from a distance or floating above their bodies and looking down at them. They can describe feeling as if their body does not belong to them, as though they are playing a role or that they have become robotic.

+ *Derealisation* – feeling as if the world or others around you are unreal or unfamiliar. Some people say that things seem distant or foggy, or that items seem to change size, shape, or colour. Others say the world seems cartoon-like, or that they feel trapped in a bubble.

+ *Amnesia* – causes gaps in memory and lost time, sometimes with limited or no awareness of the loss. This goes beyond ordinary forgetting and can include being unable to remember significant and important information about who you are, your name, the names of your loved ones, or where you live, as well as forgetting events and whole periods of life. Individuals may wonder "where the time has gone" – or may feel ashamed or anxious about lost minutes, hours, days, or longer – and hide that they have no recollection of the missing time.

✤ *Dissociative amnesia "with fugue"* is rare. It includes sudden, spontaneous, or purposeful travel. When it occurs, individuals are unable to remember extensive and important personal information and may assume a new identity or life.

✤ *Identity confusion* – feeling uncertain or conflicted about who you are. Individuals struggle to define who they are, to identify what interests them, or what they think, believe, want, like or dislike.

✤ *Identity alteration* – includes changeable and markedly different ways of being. Individuals may or may not be aware of these changes in presentation, but with awareness, some have described it "as though someone else is in charge of my body", and that they are "watching what is happening without being able to control or influence events or behaviour". Dramatic shifts in mood, voice tone, choice of words or language, behaviour, childlike or teenage presentations may be noticeable; individuals may also identify themselves by a different name. These changes have sometimes been called "switches", "switching" or "transitioning", and altered states have been described using various labels, including: "parts", "alters", "self-states", "ego states", "others", "insiders", "voices", "little ones" or "littles".

✤ *Somatoform Dissociation*[13] – sometimes referred to as "conversion disorder",[14] includes changes in body functions, sensations, movements, or control *that are not explained by other conditions*, and for which no cause can be identified. It can include seizures, weakness or loss of control, pain or numbness or paralysis, spontaneous movements, speech problems or difficulty swallowing, or changes in senses – including taste, smell, sound, and sight.

✤ *Other Specified Dissociative Disorder* (OSDD)[15] – includes symptoms above and causes significant distress and difficulties in managing life. Individuals may experience all the challenges and symptoms associated with DID, but *without either* amnesia or loss of overall control. Individuals with OSDD may have parts that strongly influence their moods, thoughts, and behaviours, but may also have greater self-awareness or internal collaboration.

✤ *Dissociative Identity Disorder* (DID)[16] – includes the symptoms above and disrupted identity *with two or more parts of self*, causing loss in a sense of self across time.

DID also occurs on a scale elaborated in the structural model of dissociation.[17, 18] This model identifies three levels of dissociation occurring in degrees of complexity, relative to more severe and/or prolonged traumatisation.

Primary dissociation includes *one Apparently Normal Part* (ANP) who tends to take responsibility for everyday life, and *one Emotional Part* (EP) who remembers or "holds" the traumatic memories and accompanying beliefs or responses. EPs may remain stuck, the same age as when the individual was traumatised, and often believe they are still living through those times, as if still in the "trauma time". As a result, they are often triggered by reminders of the trauma, and reliving experiences.

Secondary dissociation includes *one* ANP and *two or more* EPs.

Tertiary dissociation includes *two or more* ANPs and *at least two* EPs.

The picture book introduces us to "our child" who represents the ANP, whom the book and this guidebook refer to as the *"everyday self"*.[19] The picture book also introduces EPs, whom the book and this guidebook refer to as *"parts"*. When reflecting on a divided structure of personality, the everyday self or selves (ANPs) may also be considered "parts".

> Don't assume everyone is the same inside, and don't assume there will only be a few parts
> (Jennifer & Parts)

DID: making sense of it all

When experiences overwhelm our abilities to cope, when safety is inaccessible or recovery is unachievable, memory encoding is disrupted. Elements of memory are split away, they are "dissociated" and fragmented, beyond deliberate retrieval.[20] This generally occurs outside of conscious control, and may be essential for an individual's survival, their ability to cope, or the need to carry on with daily life as if everything is normal.

In severe conditions, the strength or accumulative nature of dissociated memory may form *divided parts of self*,[21] as observable in DID.[22] These parts retain a distinct sense of self or identity and keep the trauma memories as part of their own apparently individual history.

Memories held by dissociated parts can be accurate, even though their content, sequence, or the presence of another part of self remains hidden. However, as flashbacks and enduring symptoms indicate, these psychobiological barriers are not solid. Parts and memory remain sensitive to triggering and reactivation in the form of intrusive images, sensations or emotions and seemingly inexplicable symptoms that occur in response to unconscious reminders of the trauma. When the environment is no longer dangerous or the threat of abuse has passed, the brain and "parts of self" do not spontaneously recognise the changes in conditions, nor does memory spontaneously return. Parts may continue to respond as if in "trauma time", usually staying at the same stage of development they were when dissociated, and sometimes believing they are still living in that timeframe. This causes distress, and alongside a disruption in continuous memory, it can undermine everyday life and relationships significantly.

Changes in presentation or identity may occur when different parts are activated. They may take charge of the body for a time, and later change places with another part. This is called sequential dissociation[23], and the change in presentation has sometimes been called a "shift" or a "switch". Others have described parts "going inside" and "stepping back" or "coming to the front" or "stepping forwards". When two or more parts are activated at the same time, they may share elements of awareness, memory, or control. They may retain an individual sense of self and be "co-present", or they may experience a more unified sense of self and some loss in individuation, sometimes called being "blended". Changeability may be experienced in emotion, behaviour, memory, cognition, perception, awareness, sensations, and in the way the body responds or performs.

Hearing voices is a symptom that overlaps with other conditions, including psychosis. In order to avoid misdiagnosis, it is important to distinguish the differences in the nature and degree of these symptoms,[24] which alongside other first rank Schneiderian[25] symptoms are more common in DID.[26] Some individuals with DID do not hear their parts and are unaware of them, whilst others can hear their parts but may never question that we all hear internal voices. Conversational expressions may mask these effects, "one part of me wants … but the other part of me would like …"; "my inner critic" is another familiar term. Some survivors have described hearing their parts, "hearing voices" for the first time, in their teens or adulthood and believing they were going mad. Individuals with awareness of their parts may use the pronoun "we" or refer to themselves as "plurals"; they may refer to their parts as a "team", a "system", or use other terms. They may also deliberately choose to avoid using such terms since this is open to misinterpretation by those unfamiliar with dissociation.

Parts may or may not be aware of dissociated memories or of one-another. When this is the case dissociative experiences tend to be more confusing. When parts become aware of one-another, they often experience conflict caused by conflicting aims or desires. *Co-consciousness*, when parts can observe events and share memory between themselves, helps internal communication and collaboration. As parts learn to co-operate and to work together, recovery can accelerate and self-management can improve, alongside safety and increased wellbeing.

Dissociative features in DID – through the lens of "parts"

+ *Depersonalization*: the everyday self or parts may have been triggered or "switched", affecting their experience of sensations, emotions, control of the body and/or self-perception. It is an experience that may replicate "trauma time", and without context, it is bewildering.

✦ *Derealisation*: as above, the everyday self or parts, may have been triggered or "switched", and in an altered state, they have a distorted awareness of current time and the environment. They may be unable to establish full awareness of their surroundings and experience, and perceptions seem "warped". Without internal co-operation, individuals may feel stuck and unable to change this experience, and out of context this is disorienting.

✦ *Amnesia*: the everyday self or parts may have been present for different experiences and amounts of time. Without co-consciousness or collaboration between them, memories of the experience and periods of time are not shared. Losing time and continuous memory in this manner can be highly disruptive and frightening; it can also represent risk.

✦ *Amnesia with fugue*: the everyday self or parts may find themselves in a different place with no idea how they got there. Uncommonly, a part may assume overall control of an individual and their life; without an awareness of preceding days, weeks or sometimes years, they may abruptly leave familiar environments and relationships, and begin a new life, with a different identity, sense of self, or purpose.

✦ *Identity confusion*: with or without an awareness of parts, the everyday self or parts may experience a fluctuating sense of self, and changeability in their likes and interests. When co-consciousness or an awareness of other parts of self is absent or only partial, a varied or contradictory experience of self and the world results.

✦ *Identity alteration*: occurs when different parts of self are activated and in charge of the body, behaviours, and presentation. Some individuals and parts can suppress or conceal these changes, especially when it is crucial to their wellbeing or the wellbeing of others, or when their environment requires them to assume responsibility or to behave more formally, e.g., when at work. When not masked, these changes are often significant and observable.

✦ *Somatoform dissociation*: components of memory including physical sensations and physical responses to the trauma may "replay" when parts are present or triggered, or when elements of memory breach dissociative barriers. They may be experienced as medically inexplicable symptoms, sensations or as a lack of expected sensations or control.

Severe and continuing abuse, especially organised forms of abuse, tends to have themes of torture and sadism. Survivors may divide or fragment many times during these experiences to endure or to stay alive. This produces "polyfragmentation", when an individual may have tens or many hundreds of different parts and an internal hierarchy that obeys abusers' conditioning and instructions. This form of fragmentation is called *quaternary dissociation*[27] and came to public attention in the first landmark court case[28] of its kind in 2019. Features of DID that indicate possible organised abuse are noted in Chapter 3: Treatment.

Notes

1   van der Kolk, B.A., McFarlane, A.C. & Weisaeth, L. (Eds.), 1996. *Traumatic stress: The effects of overwhelming experience on mind, body and society*. New York: Guilford Press; Putnam, F.W. (1985). Dissociation as a response to extreme trauma, in R.P. Kluft and American Psychiatric Association. *Childhood antecedents of multiple personality*. Washington, DC: American Psychiatric Press; van Dijke, A., Ford, J.D., Frank, L.E. & van der Hart, O., 2015. Association of childhood complex trauma and dissociation with complex posttraumatic stress disorder symptoms in adulthood. *Journal of Trauma & Dissociation*, 16(4), pp. 428–441.

2   Nijenhuis, E. & van der Hart, O., 2011. Dissociation in trauma: A new definition and comparison with previous formulations. *Journal of Trauma & Dissociation*, 12(4), pp. 416–445; Dorahy, M.J. & van der Hart, O., 2015. DMS-Vs posttraumatic stress disorder with dissociative symptoms: Challenges and future directions. *Journal of Trauma & Dissociation*, 16(1), pp. 7–28.

3   "Dissociation is conceptualized as a basic part of the psychobiology of the human trauma response: a protective activation of altered states of consciousness in reaction to overwhelming psychological trauma", p. 312. Loewenstein, R.J., 1996. Dissociative amnesia and dissociative fugue, in L.K. Michaelson & W.J. Ray (eds), *Handbook of dissociation: Theoretical, empirical, and clinical perspectives* (pp. 307–336). New York, NY: Plenum; Haddock, D.B. (2001) *The dissociative identity disorder sourcebook*. McGraw-Hill Companies, Inc: USA.

4   Excellent information is available from Blue Knot: www.blueknot.org.au/resources/publications/trauma-and-memory.

5   van der Kolk, B. & Fisler, R., 1995. Dissociation and the fragmentary nature of traumatic memories: Overview and exploratory study. *Journal of Traumatic Stress*, 8(4), pp. 505–525.

6   An excellent graphic is available at NICABM: www.nicabm.com/trauma-how-trauma-can-impact-4-types-of-memory-infographic/?del=homepageinfographics (accessed 17/1/21).

7   Dalenberg, C.J., Brand, B.L., Gleaves, D.H., Dorahy, M.J., Loewenstein, R.J., Cardeña, E., Frewen, P.A., Carlson, E.B. & Spiegel, D., 2012. Evaluation of the evidence for the trauma and fantasy models of dissociation. *Psychological Bulletin*, 138(3), pp. 550–588.

8   Ehlers, A. & Clark, D., 2000. A cognitive model of posttraumatic stress disorder. *Behaviour Research and Therapy*, 38(4), pp. 319–345.

9   Brewin, C.R., 2018. Memory and forgetting. *Current Psychiatry Reports*, 20(10), p. 87; Ghetti, S., Edelstein, R.S., Goodman, G.S., Cordòn, I.M., Quas, J.A., Alexander, K.W., Redlich, A.D. & Jones, D.P., 2006. What can subjective forgetting tell us about memory for childhood trauma? *Memory & Cognition*, 34(5), pp. 1011–1025.

10   Sar, V., Dorahy, M. & Kruger, C., 2017. Revisiting the etiological aspects of dissociative identity disorder: a biopsychosocial perspective. *Psychology Research and Behavior Management*, 10, pp. 137–146.

11   See note 2.

12 Listed in the ICD-11, and the DSM-V.

13 Nijenhuis, E.R.S., 2009. Somatoform dissociation and somatoform dissociative disorders, in P.F. Dell & J. O'Neil (eds), *Dissociation and dissociative disorders: DSM-IV and beyond,* (pp. 259–277). New York: Routledge, available at: www.enijenhuis.nl/sdq (accessed 6/11/20).

14 ISSTD, Fact Sheet IV: "What are the dissociative disorders?" available at: www.isst-d.org/public-res ources-home/fact-sheet-iv-what-are-the-dissociative-disorders/ (accessed 14/11/20).

15 See the ICD-11, 6B6Y and/or the DSM V, 300.15, (Unspecified DD 300.16).

16 See the ICD-11, 6B64 and/or the DSM V, 300.14 (F44.81).

17 Hart, O., Nijenhuis, E. & Steele, K., 2006. *The haunted self.* New York: Norton; Nijenhuis, E., van der Hart, O. & Steele, K., 2010. Trauma-related structural dissociation of the personality. *Activas Nervosa Superior*, 52(1), pp. 1–23. It is beyond the scope of this book to elaborate all the models of dissociation. The reader may wish to research these models, including integrative systems perspectives, neurobiological models, the sequential model, the ego state model, the BASK model and cognitive behavioural approaches to dissociation.

18 Colin Ross has proposed a more inclusive modification of this theory. He recommends that structural dissociation could become one category within a broader theory of dissociation and its presentations. See Ross, C., 2017. *Structural Dissociation: A Proposed Modification of the Theory*, Kindle preview).

19 This "self" is part of the whole but may assume a greater role due to their more frequent presence as they handle daily life. In her book, *Healing the Fragmented Selves of Trauma Survivors* (2017; Routledge), Janina Fisher refers to this self as the "going on with normal life part", and in the *Structural Model of Dissociation*, van der Hart, Nijenhuis and Steele, refers to this self as the "apparently normal part".

20 Brewin, C.R., 2018. Memory and Forgetting. *Current Psychiatry Reports*, 20(10), p. 87.

21 In different models, some of the names given to dissociated parts have included "self-states", "ego states", "alter personalities", "emotional parts", "modules" and "identity states". Other less clinical names used by those familiar with DID also include "insiders", "littles", "the system" "the gallery", "voices", as well as individual names and others less genial.

22 DSM V, 300.14 (F44.81): Diagnostic and Statistical Manual of Mental Disorders, 5th Edition: DSM-5 (2013). Washington, DC, USA: American Psychiatric Publishing.
ICD-11, Dissociative Identity Disorder 6B64, available at: https://icd.who.int/browse11/l-m/en#/http %3a%2f%2fid.who.int%2ficd%2fentity%2f108180424 (accessed 14/11/20).

23 Nijenhuis, E.R.S & van der Hart. O., 2011. Dissociation in trauma: A new definition and comparison with previous formulations. *Journal of Trauma and Dissociation*, 12(4), pp. 416–445; Danylchuk, L.S. & Connors, K.J., 2016. *Treating complex trauma and dissociation: A practical guide to navigating therapeutic challenges.* New York: Routledge, Chapter 2.

24 Brand, B.L. & Loewenstein, R.J., 2010. Dissociative disorders: An overview of assessment, phenomenology and treatment. *Psychiatric Times*, 62–69, p. 67.

25 Including "hearing voices" (inner dialogues, commenting, reproaching, crying or screaming), "thought insertion" (unfamiliar thoughts occur unexpectedly) or thought withdrawal (when the mind suddenly goes blank or words seem to be snatched away), "delusions" (of the body being influenced or controlled; that feelings, sensations, impulses, or actions are influenced or generated by someone else), "hallucinations" (intrusive images, often related to trauma, where reality testing generally remains intact).

26 Ross, C., 2004. *Schizophrenia: Innovations in diagnosis and treatment*. New York: Haworth Press; Moskowitz, A., Schafer, I. & Dorahy, M. (eds), 2008. *Psychosis, trauma and dissociation: Emerging perspectives on severe psychopathology*. New York: Wiley; Steele, K., Boon, S., & van der Hart, O., 2017. *Treating trauma-related dissociation, a practical, integrative approach.* London: WW Norton & Co Ltd, pp. 104–108.

27 Sinason, V., 2020. *The truth about trauma and dissociation: Everything you didn't want to know and were afraid to ask*. UK: Confer Books.

28 Haynes, Jeni, 2019. Dissociative identity disorder: The woman who created 2500 personalities to survive. *BBC News*, 6 September, available at: www.bbc.co.uk/news/world-australia-49589160 (accessed 28/8/20).

3 Treatment

One size does *not* fit all

Various therapy models and theories elaborate the development of dissociative disorders, but the therapeutic relationship is foundational to effective treatment in all, and trust is a critical element. The complexities of fragmentation and the different histories experienced by survivors *and their part*s, means that what works for one individual, *or for one part of an individual*, may be frightening or inappropriate for another. Concepts and interventions must inform, but not take precedence. We must not "do" therapy, but instead offer insight, and make use of theories and interventions to serve clients.

> The most fundamental tool in the therapy tool kit is the relationship between
> client and therapist where secure attachment can be actioned.
>
> (Michele & Parts)

Survivors have long histories of needing to please others which will affect their approach to therapy. With DID and OSDD, it is likely that parts will feel conflicted, some wanting to please the therapist, some afraid of failure, some afraid of vulnerability or exposure, others highly defended or even hostile to engaging with the therapist at all. Any approach to treatment must take into account both the needs *and preferences* of a client *and their parts*, the skill set of a practitioner, and the desired treatment goals.

Individuals with a history of complex, interpersonal trauma and dissociative difficulties frequently enter therapy struggling with comorbid disorders, including depression, anxiety, eating disorders, substance abuse and somatoform disorders. Diagnosis of dissociative disorders (DD) is often delayed due to a lack of clinical awareness and/or screening for dissociation, and as a result many have previously received multiple diagnoses including Emotionally Unstable Personality Disorder, Bipolar Disorder and/or Psychosis.[1] Since accurate assessment affects treatment and recovery, it is beholden upon the professional community to gather adequate training to avoid perpetuating this situation. When DD are overlooked, recovery is hindered, as treatment either fails to be effective or gains are not sustained. When this happens, therapists can lose confidence in their ability to help, or they may assume too much responsibility and simply work harder to deliver desired outcomes. Sadly, and destructively, survivors may be blamed for not trying hard enough, or for being resistant or even untreatable. Both parties can feel helpless and stuck. If you recognise these scenarios, be reassured that dissociation IS treatable.

DOI: 10.4324/9781003148128-4

Assessment

Therapists who are unfamiliar with assessments, or those who prefer to step away from a more medical framework, may be reluctant to use standardised assessments. A conversational approach may initially provide sufficient information if a practitioner is familiar with the presenting issues and problems and knows what questions to ask to elaborate understanding. However, assessments that have been tried and tested for screening and scaling problems may provide insights faster, and as a result of skilled development and standardisation, can provide clarity about the severity or complexity of difficulties. We want GPs to correctly identify the nature of illness since accurate diagnosis is critical to treatment and outcome. The same might be said of assessment in mental health, and in the treatment of complex disorders *"assessment is of major importance"*.[2]

Assessment and screening can help professionals and clients ensure a "good fit" for working together, both in competence and relationship, and is meant to be a two-way process. Whilst a professional may use screening or assessment questionnaires to help them understand the nature or degree of a client's difficulties, the client may assess a practitioner's manner and approach to sharing information and control of the process. Assessment enables us to ask, *"what happened to this individual?"*, and helps us make sense of current difficulties. Implemented well, it can support a partnership between a therapist and a client who may be *unable* to "fit in" to protocols and processes. There is more information on screening and assessment in Chapter 4: Supporting practitioners.

When amnesia is featured, clients may attend therapy with problems that are significant in intensity and/or number, but without an awareness of the source or cause. Whilst symptoms may indicate a trauma history, amnesia occurs for good reason; practitioners will need to exercise care and caution, and to avoid probing hidden histories or making pronouncements about suspected abuse. Treatment does *not* depend on a client's ability to remember.

The first five items on this checklist are representative of dissociative disorders. The presence of additional items listed indicates the greater likelihood of a dissociative disorder and the importance of screening for dissociation:

☐ Memory variations, lost time, or amnesia

☐ Identity confusion or alteration

☐ Derealisation – feeling the world or others are unreal or unfamiliar

☐ Depersonalization – feeling disconnected from your body or emotions

☐ Somatoform or conversion disorders

☐ Repeated or ongoing trauma, including interpersonal, war and natural events

☐ Multiple or varied diagnoses

☐ Long-term association with mental health provision

☐ Childhood trauma

☐ Many adverse childhood experiences (ACEs)

More information about the continuum of dissociation and dissociative disorders is provided in Chapter 2: Dissociation – a continuum.

Important differentiations

Understanding and differentiating between single-incident and repeated trauma is essential in treatment.

⬇ PTSD may occur after experiencing or witnessing a threat to life, serious injury or violence – *as the result of a "single-incident" trauma.*

It is normal to experience symptoms of shock for up to one month after a traumatic experience. PTSD is diagnosed if those symptoms fail to reduce or persist beyond that point, and "delayed-onset PTSD" may be diagnosed if they develop later.
Symptoms include:

☐ intrusive memories – images, replaying like a movie, and nightmares

☐ hypervigilance, exaggerated startle responses and sensitivities, poor sleep

☐ avoidance – of subjects or places

☐ negative changes in thinking or mood, poor concentration

⬇ Complex PTSD (CPTSD)[3] – *occurs as a result of repeated trauma.* Most often interpersonal in nature, it may result from deliberate abuse, neglect, rejection, or abandonment; medical procedures may also be contributory.
Symptoms *may* include those present in PTSD[4] and:

☐ negative beliefs about self and poor self-image

☐ difficulties managing and coping with unpredictable emotions and behaviours, eg: expressing emotions, feeling suicidal, depressed, anxious, ashamed, misplaced guilt, self-harming

☐ relationship problems and disruptions, difficulties trusting, wanting to withdraw, vulnerability to unhealthy relationships

☐ altered sense of self

☐ dissociation: *not knowing who you are and feeling bad about yourself, feeling worthless, bad, or damaged; feeling unreal, detached or as if the world around you is unreal or distant; memory problems, blanking out, difficulty concentrating*

It may also include:

☐ limited impulse control

☐ substance abuse, alcohol, drugs or food

☐ panic attacks or other anxiety disorders

☐ somatoform disorders, unexplained pains, migraines, stomach problems, low energy, fatigue

☐ antisocial behaviour

☐ obsessive-compulsive difficulties

☐ phobias

☐ loss of control, trance states

☐ long-term mental health involvement

When traumatic conditions endure, an individual's psychological, physical, and social development is damaged. When harm is caused by those who should take care of us, through deliberate action or neglect, and when natural longings for comfort and care are met with pain or rejection, the conflict experienced can be intolerable. Without the ability or power to take charge of their own needs or environments, children cannot cope with knowing what they know, nor feeling what they feel. Dissociation may occur because an individual's ability to integrate experiences is reduced, or as a defence mechanism.

⬦ DID includes symptoms of PTSD and CPTSD and is further distinguished by:

☐ derealisation

☐ depersonalisation

☐ amnesia/time loss, memory variations

☐ identity confusion/alteration

☐ two or more parts/self-states

It may also include:

☐ somatoform dissociation

☐ loss of control, trance states

☐ hearing voices or hallucinations

♦ DID Features *indicative of possible organised abuse*,[5] as above, may include:

☐ polyfragmentation (tens and hundreds of parts/self-states),

☐ more than one internal hierarchy and/or elaborate internal structures

☐ parts trained by abusers to fulfil designated roles or "jobs"

☐ parts who believe they are demons, aliens or animals

☐ severe dysregulation related to significant dates (birthdays, holidays, religious festivals)

☐ conditioned and/or automatic responses

☐ severe/intractable depression and suicidality

☐ seemingly bizarre intrusions and nightmares

☐ artwork portraying torture or severe abuse

☐ sudden and severe pain or spasms when approaching trauma material

☐ severe and unusual phobias

Working with survivors of organised abuse is particularly challenging. It is strongly recommended that practitioners ensure they complete specialist training for this work and contract with an appropriately trained and experienced professional for supervision.

Which treatment model?

The experience of trauma and abuse lodges in the mind *and* the body. It is generally stored without context and separate from the awareness of working memory. The individual becomes the trauma site, and symptoms and presenting problems are expressions of the traumatic experience. When reactivated or triggered, these experiences "replay" through *seemingly* unprovoked symptoms – physical sensations, mental and emotional distress, and behavioural disruptions. Without treatment or resolution, they keep individuals anchored to the past and stuck in "trauma time".

Responses to natural disasters include rescue, containment, assessment, stabilisation, and restoration. The aim is to protect life, improve health, support morale, and enable recovery. Disaster responses are holistic – physical, practical, social, mental, and emotional and the same is required for recovery from interpersonal trauma and abuse. It is important to review treatment frameworks, models, and interventions through the lens of trauma and dissociation and thereafter to skilfully integrate therapies and interventions.

Different models can approach the same difficulties in significantly different ways. Somatic approaches focus on the body and are often referred to as "body-based" or "bottom-up" approaches. Cognitive approaches focus on mental processes, thoughts, and behavioural patterns, and are referred to as "top-down" approaches; creative therapies enable exploration and story-telling unhindered by language or self-focus.

> Given the multiplicity of the client with DID, a multiple treatment approach is necessary, as what works and feels safe for one part, might be threatening to another ... *it is imperative treatment consists of what feels doable to the client and [her/his] parts.*
> (Michele & Parts)

Bottom-up processing

Trauma impacts the way in which the brain develops and works. It is primarily stored implicitly, in physical or emotional states, and often lacks a clear narrative. During a traumatic experience certain parts of the brain decrease, inhibiting access to cognition and thought and shutting down the parts of the brain (Broca's area[6]) required to make sense of things and to communicate them. Trauma processing can retrigger the same responses evoked by the trauma, even causing individuals to be unable to speak or find words to express themselves and making the curious stance required for top-down approaches inaccessible.

The language of the body is not verbal, instead it communicates through its health, symptoms, and sensations. Even in the absence of explicit memory or specific recollections, engaging with the implicit narrative told by the body enables healing and recovery.

Somatic and bottom-up approaches help individuals learn how to pay attention to the imprint trauma has left on the body. These approaches help individuals learn the body's language and to engage with the story it tells through nonverbal physical states, emotions, relational habits, or responses. Gently and compassionately, individuals can develop a repertoire of resources and skills for calming the body, soothing emotions, and resolving traumatic memory without needing to talk about their experiences.

Top-down processing

Cognitive and top-down approaches use our capacities for observation, curiosity, and awareness.

Individuals learn how to pay attention to internal cognitions, (thought processes and imagery), emotions, and behavioural patterns. They identify strategies that may have once been helpful, but which in current life may be maintaining problems. Once identified, individuals can be supported to create alternative, more adaptive responses.

Traumatic memory is resolved through imaginal reprocessing or exposure. Individuals receive information that enables them to challenge misperceptions and to correct or replace distorted thoughts with healthy and supportive beliefs. They learn about self-compassion, and practice self-soothing techniques, problem-solving and relationship skills. They are able to look back and understand that the child they were cannot be held responsible nor blamed for traumatic events; they can look forwards and learn that they are able to create safety and stability, to live without fear, and to feel good about themselves.

To resolve the imprint of trauma and its legacies, both bottom-up and top-down approaches are necessary.

Creative therapies and approaches are helpful when talking is difficult, and when focusing attention on the body may be too challenging. Art, clay, sand, play-figures, puppets, storytelling, role-play, or music can help clients to express themselves, to bypass internal rules and expectations, and to bear witness to unconscious themes. Creative approaches can be invaluable for providing insight, release, and resolution.

Treatment decisions: "what", "how" and "when"

These are better managed in collaboration *with* a client. The therapist may bring skill and understanding, but must work responsively to the needs of the individual and their parts who are experts on their own experience. Developing a repertoire of knowledge and skills is necessary since different parts may have different preferences and capacities for engaging with different models and ways of working.

> Patience is key in the treatment of DID; what might seem like an excellent way
> forward to the therapist might require time for the system.
>
> (Michele & Parts)

Establishing rapport and engaging support through care and respect for each part may model co-operation to parts who hold opposing roles or ambitions and bring balance to conflicting aims or goals. It is possible for parts to be unaware of one-another or to hold back from engaging in therapy, usually for significant reasons; some parts may choose to remain hidden whilst others may exert influence over the work implicitly or explicitly. Different modalities may enable them to approach the work with greater ease or confidence.

A phased approach

A phased approach to treatment was proposed by Judith Herman in 1992[7] and is recommended by experts familiar with complex trauma. It recognises the complexities and challenges of working with survivors of chronic and severe trauma, whose cumulative history may mean they lack the resources required to engage in treatment without further decompensation or retraumatisation. A staged plan provides strategy and containment for practitioners and clients who may share conflicting aims; it can help resolve potential tensions between desires to recover whilst also striving to avoid potentially overwhelming material or emotions.[8]

A three-phase model is clearly presented in the ISSTD[9] Treatment Guidelines and endorsed in the ISTSS[10] Guidelines for treating Complex Trauma[11] (further sources of information are listed in Chapter 7: Additional resources). As a roadmap for treatment, the model supports a therapeutic journey that requires planning, preparation, repetition, and reflection – one that may include false starts, lay-bys, doubling back and necessary detour.

The phases of treatment are interrelated and overlapping, but also ordered and hierarchical. Whilst valuable critique reaffirms the need for contextualisation and adaptation, particularly for survivors for whom stabilisation may prove elusive[12], checklists are offered here as prompts for the tasks and processes involved in a phased approach.

Safety and relationship are key and underpin every phase of the work.

Phase I: Safety, stabilisation, and resourcing

Cues of safety are the treatment.[13]
Safety and stabilisation – safety and stabilisation – and repeat …

Whilst we want to avoid unwarranted delays in processing, we would not try to debrief a soldier in the midst of battle, nor should we try to work on trauma memories if the client's world is still unsafe, or if they cannot achieve stability. A safe therapeutic relationship is a prerequisite.

Key elements of this phase include establishing reliable and predictable boundaries – in the therapeutic relationship, in the sessions and in the intervening time.

Some parts cannot understand time, so that "between sessions" can feel like months, not mere days.
(Jennifer & Parts)

Trust cannot be assumed and may take a long time to establish. Clients and parts need to experience constancy, empathy, attunement, openness, non-judgemental curiosity, and genuine care in order to internalise a healthy capacity for attachment, and to give up suicidal and self-destructive behaviours.

Developing a shared understanding about difficulties and agreeing the process of therapy is critical to establishing an alliance that will increase the likelihood of successful outcomes. A wide range of goals include: information sharing (psychoeducation); clarifying expectations; planning for potential crises; identifying triggers and reactions; teaching self-soothing and grounding skills; developing distress tolerance; emotional regulation; positive coping strategies and problem-solving skills – all to promote stability and conditions that ultimately need to be reproduced *within* the client.

Interaction with parts helps to foster understanding and supports therapeutic goals, co-consciousness, internal acceptance, and collaboration.

> If parts give you their names, please use them. Don't just use the name of the everyday person … but also don't ask for names. Names give power to those that know them. Give us permission not to give a name and to not come if asked for.
>
> (T & Parts)

Younger parts can appear early in treatment, seeking comfort or attachment. It is usually better to equip adult parts to take responsibility for their needs to avoid triggering more guarded or hostile parts.

Successful achievement of Phase I goals may be enough for some individuals as they begin to understand themselves better, develop greater internal collaboration and more control over their daily life and experiences. Individuals who lack resources, socially, financially, or emotionally may be unable to continue therapy, in which case the work should focus consistently and entirely on stability and skills to manage crises and symptoms. It is hoped clients will be able to continue towards healing, rather than simply coping. If therapy continues, the skills and strategies developed in this phase are crucial to every phase of the work and will be returned to many times before the work is completed.

Checklist Phase I: safety and stability

☐ Enquiry/referral and intake:

- ■ Safety and relationship building are prerequisites, with attention to attunement and mutual understanding

- ■ Screening and assessments

- ■ Clarifying expectations and boundaries, including consideration of possible dependence challenges, phobic avoidance or resistance

☐ Safety

- ■ Assessing daily life challenges and risk management strategies, identifying triggers and responses, crisis planning and coping strategies, self-soothing, affect tolerance and grounding skills

- ■ Networking where possible and with client agreement, with other practitioners or support providers, including the client's GP and mental health team

☐ Stability

- ■ Considering current circumstances, social and practical support

- ■ Psychoeducation and shared understanding

- ■ Addressing problem-solving skills, positive coping skills, and facilitating safe expressions of emotion and attachment – internally and externally

- ■ Creating collaboration and planning for possible therapeutic ruptures or difficulties

☐ Review and collaborate on treatment aims *with* the client *and* their parts

☐ Potential ending with relapse prevention interventions and planning

Phase II: Processing memories and mourning losses

Processing traumatic experiences, implicitly and explicitly, incorporates them into memory as well as relegating them to the past. Reactivity to traumatic material is reduced, and negative emotional and behavioural responses are diminished. As individuals are able to create a coherent narrative, losses can be mourned and meaning-making can be introduced.

This can be the most challenging phase of the work, and the strength and reliability of the therapeutic relationship is critical, alongside an emphasis on internal co-operation and increasing co-consciousness. Planning and pacing are vital to avoid retraumatisation or overwhelm and sharing understanding and agreeing the process with clients is essential. It is important to balance concerns about client's readiness, against possible decompensation caused by delaying too long. It is also important to avoid working with memories intensively, session after session. Clients need time to handle grief and losses as they heal, expressing sorrow not only about what happened, but also about what they missed out on as a result. They need time to adjust their understanding and to create new meaning.

Issues of shame, powerlessness and avoidance are common, and core to dissociation. Understandably, parts represented by different genders, ages, needs or goals, by varied perspectives, recollections, and attitudes, will engage with the work with differing levels of ability and challenge. To avoid overwhelming the client, information and techniques can only be introduced when they, *and* their parts, are aware and ready to cooperate. If unhealthy coping strategies re-emerge, it is better to slow the pace of the work and to reintroduce a focus on safety and stabilisation.

Some parts may have limited understanding about "sharing" the body or being part of a "system". A healthy therapeutic relationship is necessary to model how to listen inside, to acknowledge other parts and to learn to listen to them, and to negotiate conflicts with sensitivity.

As this phase continues, it is likely that aspects of memory will increasingly emerge, and will need to be drawn together, including emotions and sensations. Parts will need to contribute portions of memory they have held, sometimes to fill gaps in sequence or context and to develop a more complete personal history that makes sense. If denial or disavowal occurs, great care must be taken to avoid imposing information or opinion and to respect those parts, who will have goals and needs attached to that stance.

When multiple or ongoing traumatic events have occurred, it is not helpful nor necessary to work with every experience. Individuals may instead choose to work with themes, or to select memories that are representative of others with overlapping experiences or feelings. It may also be beneficial to work with smaller segments of memory, in effect titrating the process to help clients manage their emotional responses, or to select and amplify positive learning. This work can also enable clients to recognise and build inner strengths and ingenuity, to create hope and greater resources.

Checklist Phase II

Internal communication and collaboration is necessary for recovery; remembering is not.

☐ Safety and relationship building/maintenance

☐ Processing – using appropriate therapeutic models, pacing, and titrating the work

☐ Working with parts, with themes, with the body, sensations, and emotions, making sense of, and integrating memory

☐ Working with intense emotions, expression, comfort and containment

☐ Working with beliefs, identifying lies and truth, introducing healthy adaptive beliefs

☐ Mourning losses and finding and/or creating meaning

☐ Review; potential ending with relapse prevention interventions and planning

Phase III: Integration, consolidation, and reconnection

Integration occurs at different levels and according to client's goals and abilities. Ultimately it is intended to generate harmony in whatever form the client and their parts agree is better. Integration allows individuals to know what was unknowable, to feel their pain and to let it settle in the past, to develop a stronger sense of self and the ability to live in the present with full awareness. With resolution of memory, they are no longer controlled by, nor anchored to, their trauma nor to abusive relationships. Some clients address gaps in memory to develop a more coherent sense of self and history; some develop increased internal co-operation to improve daily life; some choose to blend parts in order to reduce dividedness and to develop a more unified sense of self, whilst others consider blending undesirable.

This phase consolidates and increases gains made in Phase II, and often includes a greater emphasis on meaning, purpose, problem-solving and life-skills. When treatment has continued over a long time, the energy that was previously used to manage the effects of trauma, or that was invested in recovery, is available for present life and for re-imagining the future.

Checklist Phase III

Integration of memory and reconnecting with purpose.

☐ Safety and relationship maintenance

☐ Developing increased self-compassion

☐ Reconciling to the past

☐ Possible reshaping of identity through internal cooperation

☐ Possible merging (fusion) of parts IF desired by the client and their parts

☐ Enhancing life skills, including assertiveness, decision-making and autonomy

☐ Improving social skills and/or relationships

☐ Reconnecting with spirituality in a form appropriate to the client and their parts

☐ Relapse prevention and planning for ongoing support and self-development

☐ Identifying purpose, re-imagining the future

Notes

1   "Psychosis and Dissociation", presented by Colin Ross. Ivory Garden, 2016. *Psychosis and Dissociation.* YouTube. Available at: https://www.bing.com/videos/search?q=colin+ross+psychosis+you+tube& docid=608017028264494356&mid=36B3EAAFBE56A9CFDC5F36B3EAAFBE56A9CFDC5F& view=detail&FORM=VIRE (accessed 5/2/21); Waller, N.G. & Ross, C.A., 1997. The prevalence and biometric structure of pathological dissociation in the general population: Taxometric and behaviour genetic findings. *Journal of Abnormal Psychology*, 106(4), 499–510; see also note 11, in Chapter 2: Dissociation – a continuum.

2   Steele, K., Boon, S., & van der Hart, O., 2017. *Treating trauma-related dissociation, a practical, integrative approach.* London: WW Norton & Co Ltd.

3   Ford, C. & Courtois, C.A., 2012. *Treatment of complex trauma: A sequenced, relationship-based approach.* New York: Guilford Press; Salter, M. & Hall, H., 2021. *reducing shame, promoting dignity: A model for the primary prevention of complex post-traumatic stress disorder, trauma violence abuse,* forthcoming.

4   Kezelman, C.A. & Stavropoulos, P.A. (2019) *Practice guidelines for clinical treatment of complex trauma.* Blue Knot Foundation, 1.3, p. 83.

5   Miller, A., 2018. *Healing the unimaginable*, 2nd edn. New York: Routledge; Miller, A., 2018. *Becoming yourself – Overcoming mind control and ritual abuse*, 2nd edn. UK: Routledge.

6   van der Kolk, B., 2014. *The body keeps the score: Mind, brain and body in the transformation of trauma*. UK: Penguin, Chapter 3.

7   Herman, J.L., 1992. *Trauma and recovery*. New York: Basic Books.

8   Blue Knot: *Guidelines to differences between therapy for complex trauma and standard counselling approaches and guidelines to therapist competencies for working with complex trauma and dissociation* (2019) available at: www.blueknot.org.au/Resources/Publications/Practice-Guidelines/Complementary-Guidelines

9   International Society for the Study of Trauma and Dissociation. Guidelines for treating dissociative identity disorder in adults (2011), 3rd revision. *Journal of Trauma and Dissociation*, 12(2), p. 117, available at: www.isst-d.org/wp-content/uploads/2019/02/GUIDELINES_REVISED2011.pdf. [www.isst-d.org/resources/adult-treatment-guidelines/] (accessed 15/8/20).

10   International Society for Traumatic Stress Studies, *New ISTSS Preventions and Treatment Guidelines*, available at: www.istss.org/clinical-resources/treating-trauma/new-istss-prevention-and-treatment-guidelines#documents

11   Blue Knot organisation have also provided excellent resources for practitioners and supervisors. Practice Guidelines portal available at: www.blueknot.org.au/resources/Publications/Practice-Guidelines

12   Fisher, J., 2017. *Healing the fragmented selves of trauma survivors*. New York: Routledge, p. 44.

13   Porges, S., 2011. *The polyvagal theory: Neurophysiological foundations of emotions, attachment, communication, self-regulation*. New York: Norton, p. 61.

4 Supporting practitioners

Working with trauma and dissociation

Trauma treatment requires specialist training, and the more complex presentations require enhanced levels of training, understanding and experience.[1] A willingness to learn alongside the client, without assumptions, is invaluable.

> Please don't confuse your degree with our lifetime of knowledge.
>
> (A & Parts)

Please see Chapter 7: Additional resources for further information, and Chapter 5: Supporting recovery for additional insights into the parameters of the work and the questions you may need to answer for clients.

Professionals say the work is "demanding", "challenging", "confusing" and often "long-term". They also say it is the "most stimulating", "satisfying", "creative" and "immensely rewarding" work they do and find it "the greatest privilege". It requires patience, skill, empathy, professionalism and an unusual degree of honesty, humility, and persistence.

Clients may be simultaneously affected by a desire to please and by mistrust, by amnesia and by overwhelming memory. Recovery may be hard won and navigating issues of transference and countertransference, boundary issues, and the heightened risks of vicarious traumatisation are inevitable; these are not signs of failure, but normal responses to severe pain and suffering.[2]

Assessing dissociation

Some clients are reluctant to receive diagnoses because they believe they define, inhibit, or may further marginalise them; conversely others want the reassurance offered in a diagnosis, and believe it validates their difficulties, and feel relieved. The therapist's approach and manner need to bring a "lighter touch" to any such processes and reduce anxiety around them, and no client should feel under pressure to complete them.

When an individual has been severely traumatised over a long period of time, memory storage and recall is disrupted. Individuals may not remember, or have only pieces of memory, which may present only as sensations or emotions that are out of date and context and provoke confusion and distress. When clients report being unable to remember, or say that they "don't know", they are not being resistant. Instead, it may be that their defenses are stimulated to protect them from memories that are too painful to face or too

DOI: 10.4324/9781003148128-5

overwhelming to bear. Parts may be unwilling to share memories because they have assumed a protective role or because the therapeutic relationship is still very new and untested. These defenses were essential and may even have kept clients alive. Therefore, assessment[3] and treatment must foster respect, trust, pacing and patience to gather information and insights that equip, support, and empower survivors and thereafter keep in-step with what feels "doable" for the client and the client's parts.

A checklist of symptoms and presentations that indicate the likelihood of a dissociative disorder (DD) is included in Chapter 3: Treatment, and criteria for defining DD and DID are listed in both the DSM-V[4] and in the ICD-11.[5]

Screening tools

Screening tools do *not* provide a diagnosis but may help survivors and therapists work out what is going on and provide insights into the depth and complexity of difficulties. They are used to identify the *likelihood* of having a condition and may indicate further assessments are needed to make a diagnosis. However even highly validated and reliable tools have their limitations, especially when they rely on self-report. Individuals who experience amnesia, who forget that they have forgotten, may not be able to report their experiences accurately nor consistently, and may underestimate or deny their symptoms.

The most widely used tools are available online,[6] and may be downloaded free of charge for research or clinical use:

1. i. Dissociative Experiences Scale-II (DES-II)[7]

    The DES-II includes 28 self-report questions, mainly focused on psychological symptoms. It can be completed in around ten minutes and scored in less than five minutes. It screens for a wide variety of DD, including those featured in other conditions, as well as experiences that fall within the normal range, like daydreaming.

    Scores of 30 or higher represent significant dissociative symptoms and indicate further investigation may be required for diagnosis. An online search will source sites that can administer and score the assessment for you, also for free.

    ii. The DES Taxon[8] consists of eight questions, drawn from the DES-II, that have especial value when identifying significant dissociative symptoms. The DES Taxon calculator is available online, and automatically averages the score from the 8x taxon questions to provide an indication of probability regarding the presence of a significant DD.

2. Somatoform Dissociation Questionnaire[9,10](SDQ-20)

Soma refers to the body. Somatoform disorders are characterised by physical symptoms and body experiences for which there are no identifiable causes or findings. So-called *positive* symptoms are obvious and include pain or increased sensitivity to touch or tastes; *negative* symptoms refer to the absence of an expected sensation, lack of pain, numbness, or mobility or motor control. Somatoform dissociation may be represented by positive and negative symptoms.

The SDQ-20 consists of 20 self-report questions. It is straightforward to complete and helps to identify and assess the severity of different dissociative physical symptoms and body experiences. Scores of 32 or higher indicate a somatoform disorder; scores of 40 and above indicate the likelihood of a DD, with scores of 51+ suggesting the probability of DID.

The SDQ-5 consists of five questions drawn from the SDQ-20 to screen for DD.

Diagnosis

A conclusive diagnosis of a DD requires thorough assessment using structured and validated instruments. Training to administer them is recommended. They include:

1. Structured Clinical Interview for Dissociative Disorders-Revised[11] (SCID-D-R), has been proven to have good validity and is widely considered "gold standard" as a comprehensive diagnostic interview for DD. It uses open-ended questions to evaluate the presence and severity of amnesia, depersonalization, derealisation, identity confusion, identity alteration, and also acute stress disorder and trance dissociative disorder. It can take three to five hours to complete, and correlates well for treatment planning.

2. Multidimensional Inventory of Dissociation[12] (MID), is self-administered and can be used with clients aged 18 or older; there is also an Adolescent MID which was revised to be appropriate for teens. The MID consists of 218 questions that assess dissociative experiences and offers insight into the presence of five dissociative conditions including Dissociative Identity Disorder (DID), Other Specified Dissociative Disorder (OSDD), Posttraumatic Stress Disorder (PTSD), Somatic Symptom Disorder and Severe/Problematic Traits of Borderline Personality Disorder (BPD, now reclassified as Emotionally Unstable Personality Disorder, (EUPD). It takes approximately 30–60 minutes to complete, and 10 minutes to score.

3. Dissociative Disorders Interview Schedule[13] (DDIS), can be administered by a clinician or self-administered. It consists of 132 questions and is used to diagnose DD and somatic symptom disorder, borderline personality disorder and major depressive disorder. It enquires about other items relevant to DD, positive symptoms of schizophrenia, extrasensory experiences, and substance abuse. It usually takes 30–45 minutes to complete, and although there is no total score for the interview, the average scores of individuals with DID are given for each of the 16 subsections.

There is more information, *including assessments for use with children*[14] *and adolescents*[15] and treatment guidelines available online and via the ISSTD website.[16]

Measuring progress

Treating DD and DID is generally complex and non-linear. Ongoing reviews and assessments of progress are essential for prioritising, structuring, and containing the process. Screening tools may be helpful, along with other progress measures for practitioners and clients, including the "Progress in Treatment Questionnaire – Therapist" (PITQ-t) and the "Progress in Treatment Questionnaire – Patient Version", (PITQ-p).[17]

Supervision and support

Due to the controversies that have continued to surround diagnoses of DID and OSDD, practitioners may find themselves isolated within the professional community. In order to sustain a commitment to survivors of complex trauma, practitioners need to be purposeful in learning how to recognise negative effects in themselves, how to create their own support systems and how to create balance and joy for the long haul. Research has shown the benefits of supervision both in practice and to client outcomes. Ongoing supervision by a skilled and experienced practitioner is also necessary for therapist resilience, for learning, support, and wellbeing.

In order to avoid harm and to avoid professional and personal burnout or compassion fatigue, practitioners need support, insight, guidance and encouragement from professionals who are familiar not only with the theories and treatment requirements, but also with the nature of the work and the particular demands it makes. The strength of the supervisory relationship is of particular importance when the content of the work challenges personal and professional values, worldviews, and beliefs.

Practitioners also need to develop professional networks and associations that help sustain them. When the work is demanding, they need supportive professional relationships and opportunities to share confidentially and honestly about their work, their fears, doubts, pain, and frustrations, in order to reduce stress and to gather emotional support. Linking with other professionals working in the same area, developing close person-to-person work friendships, finding a mentor and creating regular opportunities for connecting helps provide the grounding and energy required for the work, and to model to clients.

Compassion fatigue (CF)

When working with trauma and abuse and engaging with others' distress and disorientation, it is important to invest time and budget in self-care as well as client-focused learning. Compassion fatigue may occur more frequently in therapists working with sexually abused clients.[18] It is distinguished by negative affect and is more likely to occur when practitioners have insufficient understanding of its causes and symptoms, and when they fail to pay attention to the signs of stress and trauma in themselves. Like dissociation it occurs on a continuum, and often remains unnoticed or unaddressed until its symptoms make life or work particularly difficult.

Burnout and vicarious trauma (VT) are the two elements of CF. Burnout is characterised by feelings of unhappiness, exhaustion, overwhelm, feeling disconnected and out of touch with who one wants to be. It may also include a loss of connection with sustaining beliefs or faith. VT includes and magnifies the symptoms of burnout and is further characterised by preoccupation or intrusive thoughts of people one has helped or is helping. It may include disrupted sleep, forgetfulness, an inability to separate from one's professional life, and experiencing reminders of client's trauma. These are normal reactions to hearing traumatic stories, and do not mean a therapist has failed. However, to safeguard one's own wellbeing, therapists need to learn about these responses and to pay attention to their own selfcare in order to support themselves for this work. Trauma survivors tend to be sensitive to the risk of harming others. Practitioners help clients as well as themselves, when they learn how to take care of themselves too.

Practitioner self-care

Professional self-care is required by most therapeutic bodies and being fit to practice is a given. It may be easy to decide whether or not to work when our challenges are clear, when we are ill or have experienced a significant negative event. However, we also need to understand our vulnerabilities to CF and the ways in which we might need to personalise self-care according to varying demands, contexts, life challenges and stages, attachment styles, personality type, interests, or extraversion-introversion traits.

There are professional assessments tools that help practitioners measure their own wellbeing and quality of life,[19] and increased opportunities for learning about it and recovering from its effects, including some seminal texts.[20] An informal self-assessment developed by the author is provided at the end of this chapter. Whilst all trauma practitioners may expect to experience some symptoms listed here, they become significant by degree or number and when they represent significant changes from the norm.

Purposeful attention to self-care is necessary to balance the effects of trauma work and establishing both understanding and routine practice will be sustaining. Applying stress management interventions personally is necessary, alongside specific considerations of:

a. Boundaries – how you engage practically and emotionally.

   Good boundaries model safety and containment for both parties and create more stability for longer-term work. It is important to consider how you separate yourself emotionally and physically at the end of the day. A routine or practice that reminds you to step back from focussing on clients or work and to return to yourself and your personal life is crucial to balance.

b. Filling up – what fills you up and equips you for your work, and what fills you personally and emotionally?

It may be training, reading, or networking, it may be that you fill up in nature, in the company of good friends or family, or by developing hobbies or expressing creativity. You will need to pay purposeful attention and to invest time in these endeavours.

c. Limitations – recognising your own limitations and giving yourself permission to be limited will help you maintain compassion for yourself as well as helping you hold realistic goals.

d. Balance – personal and professional goals need balancing with realism.

It can be helpful to identify mantra individualised to your work *with specific clients*. You might note them down to remind yourself when you reflect on your work with the client. For example, "I am not responsible for … I am a guide in this work … I have done my best; tomorrow is another day". You may find it helps to update or to adapt such mantra as the work progresses.

e. Accountability – it is important to identify individuals to whom you are willing to give account, or whom you give permission to speak into your work or your life.

In some work contexts, good managers and supervisors may bring healthy enquiry and checks to both yours and the client's wellbeing; in other contexts, and environments this may be lacking. Creating a caring and supportive professional and social network, finding individuals who will check in on you, and especially connecting with other professionals who are experienced and skilful in this work may also be essential to your welfare.

Take care of yourself – you need it, and you deserve it too!

Professional Fatigue Assessment: symptoms (√ those that apply)

☐ pre-occupied – inability to let go of work issues

☐ disengaged – feeling detached

☐ loss of sense of humour – being more serious than usual

☐ withdrawing – isolation

☐ tiredness – fatigue – loss of energy

☐ difficulty concentrating or paying attention

☐ dreaming of terminating therapy/support with a client/contact

☐ irritability

☐ intolerance

☐ negative attitude to work – demoralized

☐ increased negative feelings – loss of pleasure

☐ increased frustration, anger, and/or hostility

☐ depression

☐ increased or significant pessimism

☐ decreased empathy

☐ disrupted sleep

☐ nightmares

☐ increased drinking – drinking too much

☐ increased tv watching

☐ aches and pains

☐ somatic symptoms: bowel disturbances; breathing disturbances, skin problems

☐ increased illness

☐ headaches

☐ weight/appetite change

☐ sex life affected

☐ destructive behaviour

☐ intrusive thoughts

☐ increased anxiety

☐ feeling overwhelmed

☐ increased sense of demand or threat

☐ hypervigilance – increased reactivity

☐ client/contact work/ issues encroaching on personal time

☐ perceiving clients/contacts as needing your care

☐ perceiving clients/contacts as fragile

☐ feeling special – entitled – exception to "rules"

☐ feeling inadequate/incompetent

☐ avoiding hearing client/contact's narrative

☐ denial of symptoms/difficulties

☐ increased boredom

☐ over working

☐ increased sense of burden or responsibility

☐ increased criticism – of self and others

☐ feeling unable to share openly with supervisor/manager

Notes

1 Brand, B.L., 2016. The necessity of clinical training in trauma and dissociation. *Journal of Depression and Anxiety,* 5(251), pp. 10–4172.

2 Ross, C.A. & Halpern, N., 2009. *Trauma model therapy: A treatment approach for trauma, dissociation and complex comorbidity.* Richardson TX: Manitou Communications.

3 More information on assessment is offered in Chapter 3: Treatment.

4 *Diagnostic and statistical manual of mental disorders: DSM-5* (5th edn) (2013). Washington, DC: American Psychiatric Association.

5 International Classification of Diseases, 11th Rvn: ICD-11. (2018). WHO.

6 www.isst-d.org/resources/

7 Bernstein, E.M., & Putnam, F.W. *Dissociative Experiences Scale (DES-II, English)*, available at: http://traumadissociation.com/downloads/information/dissociativeexperiencesscale-ii.pdf [www.isst-d.org/resources/] (accessed 14/8/2); Carlson, E.B. & Putnam, F.W., 1993. An update on the Dissociative Experience Scale. *Dissociation* 6(1), pp. 16–27.

8 Darryl Perry, *Dissociative Experiences Scale, (DES-II) Taxon Calculator (Excel)*, DES-Taxon-Scorer (4). xlsx available at: www.isst-d.org/resources/

9 Nijenhuis, E.R.S., Van der Hart, O., & Vanderlinden, J., 1996. *Somatoform Dissociation Questionnaire: SDQ-20 & SDQ-5*, available at: http://www.enijenhuis.nl/sdq/

10 http://www.enijenhuis.nl/sdq

11 Steinberg M., 1994. *Structured clinical interview for DSM-IV disorders.* Washington DC: American Psychiatric Press; *Interviewers Guide to the Structured Clinical Interview for DSM-IV Dissociative Disorders (SCID-D), 1994.* Washington, DC, American Psychiatric Press.

12 http://www.mid-assessment.com/. Dell, P., 2006. The Multidimensional Inventory of Dissociation: (MID): A comprehensive measure of pathological dissociation. *Journal of Trauma and Dissociation,* 7(2), pp. 77–106.

13 https://www.rossinst.com/ddis. Ross, C., 1996–2007. *The Dissociative Disorders Interview Schedule – DSM-5.*

14 E.g., Child Dissociative Checklist (CDC).

15 E.g., Adolescent Dissociative Experiences Scale (ADES).

16 www.isst-d.org/resources/

17 Schielke & Brand, available at: https://topddstudy.com/pitq.php (accessed 2/10/20).

18 Pearlman, L.A. & Saakvitne, K.W., 1995. *Trauma and the therapist: Countertransference and vicarious traumatization in psychotherapy with incest survivors.* New York, NY: WW Norton.

19 Professional Quality of Life: Compassion Satisfaction and Fatigue Version 5 (ProQOL), available at: www.proqol.org. © Beth Hudnall Stamm, 2009–2012. This test may be freely copied if (a) author is credited, (b) no changes are made, and (c) it is not sold.

20   Books:

- *The Compassion Fatigue Workbook*, by Francoise Mathieu (2012).
- *Overcoming Compassion Fatigue: A Practical Resilience Workbook*, by Martha Teater and John Ludgate (2014).
- *Help for the Helper: The Psychophysiology of Compassion Fatigue and Vicarious Trauma,* by Babette Rothschild and Marjorie Rand (2006).
- *Treating Compassion Fatigue*, by Charles R. Figley (2002).
- *Compassion Fatigue: Coping with Secondary Traumatic Stress Disorder in Those Who Treat the Traumatized*, by Charles R. Figley (1995).
- *Transforming the Pain: A Workbook on Vicarious Traumatization*, by Karen Saakvitne and Laurie Anne Pearlman (1997).

5 Supporting recovery[1]

This chapter is written *to survivors*. Individuals may photocopy it, or sections from it, for sharing with others. Professionals may use it similarly, for sharing with clients, or as a prompt in their work.

An overview

Trauma overwhelms our coping strategies and the way the mind and body process experiences and create memory – we may remember too much or too little.[2] Although our minds and bodies try to find ways of making sense of our experiences, because we are not equipped for trauma, they can get stuck, and replay some of the most distressing parts of an event over and over. Similar to a damaged recording, the track may keep jumping back and replaying the same section on a continual loop until it is repaired.

Traumatic experiences take different shapes and forms. They may be violent, dramatic, or overpowering, or they may be silent, neglectful, or covert; they can take the form of deliberate control, abuse, and harm, or they can be the loneliness or terror of abandonment or shame.

Ongoing and repeated traumatic experiences are called complex trauma. They generally represent more severe forms of abuse, especially abuse by attachment figures, that proves too much to bear and the mind and body fail to process or store them effectively. Dissociation and fragmentation occur, and parts of self may form from such experiences.[3] These parts may hold traumatic memories separate, unresolved and stuck at the point of trauma, but defending you against pain, overwhelm or collapse.

Unsettling?

It may be troubling to consider the possibility of dissociated parts within, perhaps outside of your knowledge or awareness. We are frightened by what we do not understand, and the possibility of not knowing ourselves. Alternatively, you may be aware of your parts, or an internal system of relationships and roles. There may be conflict or collaboration; you may already have begun a journey of recovery alongside one-another. I encourage you to reclaim your life and to determine how you want to live it. You may need help – you will need encouragement.

It is difficult to trust or to reach out to others when trust has been betrayed – to be open to new ideas or ways of being when life feels hazardous, and especially when it has been *predictably unsafe*. Those of you who have survived complex trauma face these challenges, and it is my hope that you will find respect, information, and support, so you can identify what feels right for you and take decisions for your wellbeing.

DOI: 10.4324/9781003148128-6

Unfortunately, film and media portrayals of trauma and dissociation have often contributed to prejudice, misinterpretation, and myth[4] – when life was already fraught with challenges! Some individuals successfully promoted a false syndrome, ironically called "false memory syndrome",[5] to support those accused of abuse. Sadly, it seems controversies will proliferate whilst those with vested interests continue to influence popular sources. Research[6] and courage is turning the tide. It is hoped this Guidebook and its companion picture book: *Our House: Making Sense of Dissociative Identity Disorder*, will encourage you, your families, friends, colleagues, and professionals. It is also hoped it will help dispel confusion and misinformation and inspire confidence that the legacy of trauma and dissociation need not extend into an unwritten future.

Recovery: safety, support and stamina

✦ ***Safety*** is a word that can evoke different meanings or feelings for survivors. It can even be triggering – so please consider what words evoke security, stability, care or wellbeing for you; if necessary, use them in place of the word "safety".

It is important to find ways to increase your safety and to avoid things that could sabotage your efforts for recovery. A therapist can help you consider these issues, and to identify what could undermine you, your parts, or your relationships with those supporting you. However, you may need or want to start with some prompts for yourself:

⬦ *External safety* refers to your current situation – where you live, and your relationships. Is your home secure? Are you able to support yourself? Are you dependent on others for support or finance for your daily needs or to engage in therapy? Do you have stable relationships or are you at risk from others? Are you in good health? Are you and your parts ready and willing to take steps required to ensure and maintain your safety? What help do you need to achieve this? [7]

⬦ *Internal safety* refers to your inner world – how you and your parts experience and manage triggers, emotions, sensations, thoughts, or other challenges to holding steady and feeling contained. Do you understand what your triggers are, and how to safely respond to them? Do you understand your emotions and how to regulate them? Do you know how to manage intrusions in your thoughts, or how to respond to sensations that are unexpected? Are you willing to learn about self-compassion, and to develop compassion for each other? Are your parts willing to engage in therapy? If not, are they willing to back up your desire to attend therapy? Are you willing to learn about one-another and to work together?

⬦ *Grounding Skills* – safely and/or stably connect you to the present. As part of the first phase of recovery, grounding skills equip you to respond to, and manage triggers and flashbacks. Developing these skills may need experimentation and practise.

Some commonly used grounding techniques may not be helpful, especially to survivors who are hypervigilant. For example, looking around the room for "x", can increase your hypervigilance, and make you less grounded.

(Jennifer & Parts)

A therapist can help you develop a toolbox of grounding skills, or you may need or want to work on this independently. Consider skills that are personal and individualized for you and for different parts, who may prefer or respond differently to various techniques. An overview and some suggestions follow. You will find some more self-help information and resources in Chapter 7: Additional resources.

Flashbacks replay experiences or elements of memory as if they are happening now.

Images, feelings, or sensations "play again", out of context but still overwhelming.

They may be likened to an unpredictable and overpowering internal assault.

They are triggered by reminders of your trauma – things you may or may not be aware of. Triggers can include external prompts: images, sounds, smells, touch or taste, and internal cues: sensations, thoughts, emotions, or impulses. It takes time and effort to identify your triggers, especially when some parts are affected by things that others experience as neutral or even safe. Amnesia may make it difficult to differentiate between current threat and past threat. Every part may be needed to discern whether or not cues are old or recent.

Internal communication is imperative so that compromise can be reached where treatment is concerned, and everyone is enabled to feel in control and safe.

(Michele & Parts)

Planning for flashbacks, learning what interrupts them and what soothes you and your parts also takes investigation; the effectiveness of interventions may depend on what has been triggered, and which parts are affected. It may be helpful to tell trusted others what helps. You may ask them to avoid particular or abrupt movements, and to ask before touching you.

You may be helped by being reminded, or reminding yourself:

> *Although this feels real, it is NOT happening now*

> *I am remembering, but I am safe now* (if this is the case)

When you have identified your triggers, and distinguished that threat is not current, you may add "*I am triggered by … I am remembering, but I am safe now*".

Choosing to soothe and calm your body and mind may feel counter-intuitive, especially if your previous strategies have included hurting yourself or taking risks. Ironically, those strategies often persist because they are effective. However, they anchor you to the past, they maintain your sensitivity to perceived threat and decrease your resources for recovery. They can also convince parts that safety is impossible or that they are still living through traumatic times. Differentiate what is helpful for you and different parts. You might try:

⌂ Breathing slowly and deeply – this can interrupt the automatic alarm signals activated in your body

⌂ Focusing on the ground beneath your feet. Touching things around you and bringing your awareness to texture and temperature, can reconnect you to safety and help you distinguish between past and present. Sometimes holding ice or sipping water have been recommended

⌂ Noticing what is real in current time, and naming those things to stimulate your brain (frontal cortex) to re-enable perspective and/or speech

⌂ Using music or rhythm to interrupt the flashback, or to soothe. Listening to non-triggering songs can also reactivate your brain and awareness of current time

⌂ Smelling something can reorient you to the present, e.g. hand lotion, coffee, or something you associate with wellbeing, comfort or safety

⌂ Safely enabling actions that were inhibited. You may need to move, to discharge energy or to complete responses that were previously blocked or inhibited – to run, to push, to shout, to scream or to cry, to release and resolve enduring trauma effects.

Grounding reconnects your awareness to present time and helps to establish a sense of stability or calm. It is sometimes called *centering*, being *centred* or *grounded*. The techniques or skills used may vary and may also vary in their usefulness. Some focus on your body, others on your mind and still others on emotions or spirituality.

Ultimately, *grounding skills need adapting for you and for your parts*. That means some parts will find helpful, techniques that other parts find challenging, and you will need alternative techniques to help them. Consider options according to what has been triggered or sensitised, and to the ages and abilities of different parts, and learn what it means to differentiate between them.

Some examples:

➤ *Physical grounding*: bring your awareness to the world around you, and to the safety achievable in the present. Focus on your current environment; to the solidity of the ground beneath your feet, to temperature and texture; to lengthening your spine and to the strength of your own body and its boundaries. Breathe – slow down – notice tension in your body and learn to relax your muscles, to calm your body and to let the tension go.

> Being asked to press our feet on the floor is triggering for some of
> us because it activates memories of foot pain.
>
> (Jennifer & Parts)

➤ *Emotional grounding*: learn to identify your emotions, to label them and to interpret the information they give you. Bring compassion to yourself and to your parts. Help them to understand that triggers can be alarming or distressing, but that you are learning how to create safety and wellbeing for them now. Discover what helps each of you to transform your emotional state – reassurance, acceptance, comfort, sound (music or nature), understanding or action.

➤ *Mental grounding*: learn which techniques help reactivate your thinking brain, rationale and perspective. You may initially need distraction techniques like counting, noticing and labelling, recitation or crosswords, and then to develop an objective observing or curious state of mind. Thoughts are not necessarily facts, so you may learn how to identify and challenge them, maybe also to reframe your beliefs with new information. It will be important to learn how to differentiate between past, present and future – between old pain and current challenges – and to develop helpful habits and skills for shaping your thoughts and the consequences to which they contribute.

➤ *Spiritual grounding*: enables you to connect to something stronger and more positive than your current world or yourself. It may take time to identify something that inspires hope, security, or purpose, but it may also be valuable to know that it is possible.

✦ **Support** can include family, friends, and professionals. Financial resources will be necessary if you decide to work with a private practitioner.

⌂ The greatest support may come from those who are able and willing to hold hope for you, and to encourage you when things are hard. Finding "your" people, whoever they are, may be crucial. Giving them sufficient information to understand some of your challenges, and some insight into what it is like to live with dissociation and inner parts will be invaluable to you both.

⌂ Professional support may be provided via referral from your GP, from the local mental health support team, or you may be able to engage with a private therapist.

Engaging with someone previously unknown will undoubtedly raise issues of trust. Trust is not a prerequisite, it is earned, and you can take all the time you need to "check out" who a person is. You and your parts may need help, support, and information before you can consider collaboration, let alone trust. As a survivor, you may tend towards pleasing others, avoiding conflict, or being passive. Listen to your instincts and take the time you need to learn what is true, what is possible, and what you and your parts need and want. It may help to have a checklist when looking for an appropriate practitioner, and to know what are positive and negative indicators:

Sample questions to ask professionals:

☐ What training and experience does the therapist have in working with trauma?

☐ How do they understand the effects of trauma and its legacies?

☐ Do they screen for dissociation and trauma, and if so how?

☐ Can they explain the difference between PTSD, Complex PTSD, Dissociation and Dissociative Disorders? Do they understand what the differences will mean for a client's treatment, their challenges and needs?

☐ Have they successfully worked with dissociative difficulties before?

☐ What treatment approaches do they use? Do they emphasise one particular model or approach to therapy?

☐ Do they develop a treatment overview and plan for the work? How do they handle goal setting and measuring progress?

☐ How do they approach the therapeutic relationship?

☐ What can you expect in sessions and how long do they last? Who will monitor the time and how are session endings managed?

☐ How do they manage contact between sessions? Emails? Texts? Calls?

☐ How much do sessions cost, how is payment made, and what is their cancellation policy?

☐ Do they have supervision for this work?

☐ You may also ask about a supervisor's training, experience, and skill in this area.

☐ How do they manage therapy endings? Would they be decided together? Would it be possible to return?

☐ Do you like them, and do they feel safe? You may want to use the questions on safe people listed in Chapter 6, Reading deeper.

A good professional will *not*:

• control, manipulate or coerce you

• rush you

• ignore your feelings or requests

- judge nor shame you

- take a superior stance

- pressure you to trust them

- over-commit

- be overly familiar

A good professional will:

- partner with you and offer you and your parts respect and enabling

- hold your interests in mind

- be honest about their experience and training, and open to your questions

- demonstrate humility, and a willingness to learn from you and with you

- offer information, balanced by good, attentive listening and attunement to you, to your parts and to your feelings

- be open to feedback, disagreement, or challenge, and provide you with opportunity and space to do that

- encourage good boundaries so that you know what you can expect

- set limits on their availability, and take time off

- help you understand what contact is okay, and what happens with cancellations or non-attendance

- be consistent.

You will learn that your feelings, your thoughts, and your rights matter.

✚ **Stamina** for the journey. You will need time and patience, a willingness to learn new things, to develop self-compassion, to reclaim your voice, and to receive encouragement.

⬠ You and your parts survived – sometimes against yours or their will or desire. Your choices were taken away from you. Dissociation was not a choice, but it did enable your survival and it will have taken great resource, skill, and cleverness to get through. Each one of you deserves respect and help to create a life that you can learn to be proud of, but it will take perseverance and determination.

⬠ Your emotions are likely to have been a source of pain and threat. When you were young or helpless, you or some of your parts are likely to have considered them to be signs of weakness and may have found them intolerable. It may have been essential to suppress them or to ignore them; in doing so, it is likely that you dissociated further, and that some parts carried and bore the unresolved feelings as part of themselves.

The responses and attitudes that were essential when you were young or helpless, are unlikely to provide the solutions you need now that you are older or have more resources. Those earlier strategies go past their "sell by" date, and without new information or an awareness that safety and autonomy may be achievable, earlier plans of action, behaviours and responses can become unhelpful and inhibit recovery. Some selves have an almost phobic desire to avoid feelings, so it is important to learn that emotions can inform and help you in recovery. They are signals, helping you identify what you need and telling you if something is wrong or right. "Follow your feelings to find the meanings".

- Learn about your feelings and the parts who hold them

- What are they telling you?

- What did they mean once, and what might they mean now?

- How could they be helping you?

- How can you respond helpfully to them and the parts who hold them?

⌂ Your body is likely to have borne the pain, the shame, and the ongoing effects of trauma. As a result, you and your parts may feel hatred towards or have disdain for it. You may feel angry that it survived. You may want to disown it, to hurt it, to ignore it or to use it without regard for safety or care, and that may even seem instinctive.

Recovery includes learning self-compassion and self-care – even if that seems to go against the rules or seems counter-intuitive. Your body needs safety and nurture, so that it can provide safety and nurture.

⌂ "Resistance" is not resistance – it may be dissociating, protecting, forgetting, avoiding, resourcing, creating safety and boundaries. It may represent strength. When you have been overpowered by circumstances and others too strong to defy, resistance is a valuable element of recovery. It is not wrong; it helps reclaim your rights. When you or parts want to resist, experiment with that ... play with it ... explore it ...

- What is it doing for you? What does it do for other parts?

- Does it reclaim control? For whom?

- Does it pace things for you? How does that affect other parts?

- Does it validate feelings or opinions? Does it ignore others?

- Does it help? If so, how, and who does it help?

- • Is it needed indefinitely, or for a time?

- • What would you or other parts need to engage?

- • What would inspire you or other parts to try another strategy?

⌂ Distance from others is preferable when they or the world are unsafe or untrustworthy. Receiving attention may have been associated with risk. However, for the journey of recovery, you will need encouragement – from whom, or where will you draw that? Are you and your parts willing to learn how to support and encourage one-another? Are you willing to share a little more with trusted others?

> Curiosity needs to be awakened and ideas given time to be pondered and discussed internally. Confidence needs to be built in adopting new approaches, and confidence in knowing it doesn't matter if they are insurmountable or fail to help.
>
> (Michele & Parts)

Further sources of information and support are recommended in Chapter 7: Additional resources for survivors, supporters and practitioners. The ripple effects of dissociation can affect your supporters, who may sometimes struggle to know what they can do or how they can help. You may want to share the following with them:

Supporting supporters

Good, maybe familiar advice, given to anyone providing support or care includes:

➢ Look after yourself – pay attention to your own needs, to eating well, getting sufficient exercise and rest

➢ Take time for yourself, and make time for fun, friends, and hobbies

➢ Learn – the more you understand about trauma and its effects, the better equipped you will be to offer understanding and to maintain perspective. There are some reliable sources listed in Chapter 7: Additional resources

➢ Accept mixed feelings, including negative ones. They do not mean you don't love your survivor; they mean it's sometimes tough

➢ Create your own support network, from friends or family, or from professionals like your GP or from a therapist who can support you

➢ Trauma removes choice and autonomy – offer respect, and encourage independence where possible

➢ Make time to listen without expectation or judgement. Trauma, especially interpersonal trauma, produces shame, fear and secrecy, and survivors may hold back because they anticipate others will judge or criticize them

> Anxiety is a huge barrier to engaging in life, in friendships, relationships.
> Please be patient because we will get there.
>
> (Jennifer & Parts)

➢ Avoid giving advice, making demands, comparisons or telling survivors what they "should" do or feel. If it were easy, they would have managed it by now!

➢ Don't blame your struggles on the survivor's difficulties. Take responsibility for your own challenges – even if they arise in relation to the survivor – talk and negotiate

➢ Be aware of what makes the survivor feel unsafe or triggered: sights, sounds, smells or touch, dates, locations, topics of conversation, medical procedures or settings, crowds, being watched or the center of attention, unfamiliar places, public transport, surprises, or unexpected events, physical restrictions. Internal triggers might include unobserved physical sensations, hunger, thirst, tiredness or sickness, emotions, or thoughts. The survivor is not being difficult; there will be good reasons they find these things difficult that they may be unable to identify or share

➢ Trust recovers slowly. If the survivor struggles to trust you, remember it is not about you, nor can they simply decide to trust. Trust was broken, and it may take a long time to repair

➢ When the survivor is "forgetful", it may simply be that you need to say it again

> Don't assume we know something if you were communicating with another part.
> Even though it is frustrating please tell us what you need us to know even if you
> have to tell us more than once.
>
> (Jennifer & Parts)

➢ You are allowed to be limited, you will make mistakes, and you will get it wrong. You can't make things right, but you may be able to hold steady, to offer apology when you get things wrong, and to reconnect openly, honestly and kindly

➢ Celebrate gains – however small they seem. They are momentous!

➢ Be patient. Recovery is not easy.

What is it like to be many?

A small but simple example that demonstrates a difficulty faced by those with parts, managing internal conversations, may be helpful: imagine gathering two rolls of paper and two companions, and assigning yourself the goal of sharing what you did yesterday. Imagine that your two companions speak simultaneously, through the rolled tubes of paper, into your right and left ears; asking questions, singing, shouting or making critical comments; consider the challenges you might face as the speaker!

> Picture yourself in a noisy busy place where you are hearing the conversations around you but trying to
> focus intently on just one. That is how it can be for me with DID – inside my head can be like that noisy,
> busy place, speaking to someone outside can require the most tiring of attention and focus.
>
> (Jennifer)

Notes

1   Further sources of information and support are recommended in Chapter 7: Additional resources, including workbooks and some commentary on survivor forums.

2   Brewin, C.R., 2018. Memory and Forgetting. *Current Psychiatry Reports*, 20(10), p. 87.

3   Sar, V., Dorahy, M. & Kruger, C., 2017. Revisiting the etiological aspects of dissociative identity disorder: a biopsychosocial perspective. *Psychology Research and Behavior Management*, 10, pp. 137–146; Bessel van der Kolk with Tippett, K., n.d. *How trauma lodges in the body*. On being, available at: https://on being.org/programs/bessel-van-der-kolk-how-trauma-lodges-in-the-body/ (accessed 5/2/21).

4   Brand, B., Sar, V., Stavropoulos, P., Krüger, C., Korzekwa, M., Martínez-Taboas, A. and Middleton, W., 2016. Separating fact from fiction: An empirical examination of six myths about dissociative identity disorder. *Harvard Review of Psychiatry*, 24(4), pp. 257–270.

5   Although it remains unproven in science and without substantiation or acceptance in diagnostic manuals, the representation of so-called "false memory syndrome" in the public domain has sadly given it unmerited acknowledgment. For more information see: Brewin, C.R., & Andrews, B., 2017. Creating memories for false autobiographical events in childhood: A systematic review. *Applied Cognitive Psychology*, 31(1), 2–23;
Katie, H., 2021. The memory war. *The Cut*, available at: www.thecut.com/article/false-memory-synd rome-controversy.html (accessed 11/1/21).

6   Brewin, C.R., Andrews, B., & Mickes, L., 2020. Regaining consensus on the reliability of memory. *Current Directions in Psychological Science,* 29(2), pp. 121–125; Reinders, A.A.T.S. and Veltman, D.J., 2020. "Dissociative identity disorder: Out of the shadows at last?" *The British Journal of Psychiatry*, Cambridge University Press, pp. 1–2.

7   Survivors of organised or ritualised abuse experience significant challenges establishing safety. Ellen Lacter's site offers helpful insights into issues and precautions, available at: https://endritualabuse.org /topic/safety/ (accessed 27/12/20).

6 Reading Deeper

Written to survivors

In this section, we will review the images presented in the picture book, page numbers 5 to 32 and reflect on deeper meanings together. Content may be photocopied for use by practitioners.

Some of the images represent overlapping ideas, and whilst care has been taken to avoid duplicating ideas or comments, some pages offer similar information so that they can be copied for sharing and/or considered individually.

There are a few optional exercises presented by this symbol These are included to provoke further thought and to develop greater understanding. You may find it helpful to discuss these sections with someone. Please exercise your own choice and wisdom when deciding if, when, and how deeply you engage with any of them. At first glance they may seem simple or straightforward, but they may impact you deeply. Take care to work only at a level you find helpful, and at which you can maintain stability.

Please note: It is possible that different parts will have seemingly contradictory thoughts or memories about the past. This may be conflicting, especially if they relate to people who were important to you. Finding ways to accept different recollections, and to accommodate the needs that exist, will be important to your recovery.

Important point: The picture book portrays the development of DID with only *one* everyday self and several parts. Consequently, this section largely refers to only one "everyday self". However, it is important to clarify that some individuals with DID have *many* everyday selves, who help them manage different responsibilities and roles in daily life, whilst others may have only one everyday self and only one part. For more information on this and the terms used, please see Chapter 2: "Dissociation: a continuum".

<<>>

DOI: 10.4324/9781003148128-7

The foundations and building blocks of who we are, and the potential for our lives, are in place at our birth – outside of our control or choice.

Genetics dictate our gender and appearance, our physical attributes and our potential talents – our brain's potential capabilities and our potential emotional capacities – without our input or choice. *"We didn't choose ..."*

We all share the same basic needs for survival. Regardless of where we are born, who our caregivers are, or the conditions in which we grow – these needs are the same for every human being. The *provision* of our needs, *how* they are met, and the *environment* in which we grow, will shape our lives physically, mentally, emotionally, and socially. All this is outside of our control. *"We didn't choose ..."*

Outside of their awareness, children – like sponges – absorb, replicate, and respond to the beliefs, attitudes and behaviours modelled by those around them. When loved and nurtured, they can trust that their needs will be met. They can believe in a safe world and learn that they have value and meaning. When they are treated harshly, violently, or neglectfully, they must learn to take care of themselves and must develop strategies for protection and survival. They learn that their world is unsafe and must try to hide painful feelings of worthlessness and insignificance. These beliefs are sometimes deliberately taught by abusive adults so that they can behave however they want, without challenge, shrugging off their appropriate responsibilities and instilling rules of secrecy.

We all build scaffolds of belief, called "schema". Abused, traumatized or neglected children create beliefs that support and maintain some sense of control and care, to escape overwhelming feelings, helplessness, and shame. However, the truth is that infants and children do *not* have the ability to control the world around them, nor to make adults around them behave as they want or need. When we accept this truth, that *"we didn't choose"* we can begin to cast off inappropriate blame and humiliation.

We cannot change our DNA, our genetics, but we can learn how to influence their expression –
We do not choose our inheritance, but we can learn how to direct its use and influence –
This starts with understanding and acceptance, getting to know ourselves, and responding with self-compassion rather than self-criticism.

Picture book page 5: We do not choose our life

When you are born, you receive your life – you inherit and move into your house.

Its foundations represent your ancestry and your family history, to your advantage or disadvantage. Their effect on you and your inheritance were all "in place" long *before you arrived.* Its bricks and the quality of its "materials", its location, design, construction and strength were also established *before you arrived.*

The image in the picture book presents a "western" style house, brick built with deep foundations – ourselves at birth. You may find it useful to draw your own house, or one that offers a better representation of your culture; you might find or draw a picture of the house you first lived in when you were born. Alternatively, you could find or draw an image of your "baby self". Alongside careful reflection, you can use this exercise to gain new perspectives or insights into your origins and needs.

What do you know about the foundations of your house?

What have you inherited through your DNA, through your genes and your ancestry?

⌂ What ethnicity are you?

⌂ What gender are you?

⌂ What is your appearance like – height, weight, hair, and eye-colour, etc?

⌂ What is your health like?

⌂ What are your talents, and what are you good at?

⌂ What are your moods like, and how do you handle emotion?

What effects have these things had on your life, and what have they meant to you?

What might you influence?

What do you know about the building blocks of your house?

What beliefs, rules and assumptions have been built into, and shaped your life?

Can you identify them? Do you agree with them? What might you change?

Some prompts:

⌂ What did you believe about your own safety? The safety of your world?

⌂ Others' trustworthiness?

⌂ How was emotion handled, for example, were you allowed to be angry or upset?

⌂ Were you comforted, or sympathetically taught how to handle emotions?

⌂ What did you believe about your own self-worth? Did you know you were lovable?

⌂ What did you believe about your abilities, were you clever – or attractive?

⌂ Were you allowed to celebrate these things, or was it better to stay quiet about them?

⌂ What were the rules about achievement – academics, sports, creativity, social abilities?

⌂ Was it safe to be noticed, or was it important not to be noticed?

⌂ Were you compared to others, and if so, what was said? Did you believe those comments? Did you feel you had to prove them wrong or right?

⌂ What was your status in relation to your peers?
Were you able to mix and relate to those around you with confidence?

If you are working with a therapist, they may be able to add some questions here, to help you reflect on the meanings of your thoughts and answers. You may also want to consider this page alongside pages 6–10 in the picture book, and the exercises that follow here.

Picture book page 6: We do not control our environment

Our environment is likely to have a significant impact on our development. The weather system shown on this page is representative of the wider world into which we are born, including the region of the world and our country, the natural environment in which we grew, the political and economic systems that were influential on our lives and the safety we may or may not have experienced as a result.

Events outside of our control that can shape the course of our lives include wars, but also rumours of war – past or future, and natural disasters like floods, droughts or wildfires, and also the fear of these things through global warming – events that cause deprivation or fear.

Even when we are not experiencing immediate disaster, we may be affected by its impact, passed on through our DNA, through its enduring effect on our community or our caregivers, or because of the fear or shame it conjures within us and others.

 Consider the environmental influences you, and your family have experienced, including:

⟊ The region of the world and the country in which you were born and grew

⟊ The effects of the natural world on your daily life and on those around you

⟊ The political influences

⟊ The controls or liberties you experienced

⟊ The economy of the country in which you grew

⟊ The level of healthcare provision

⌂ What were the negative and positive conditions you experienced and that were experienced by those who raised you?

⌂ What effect did those conditions have on you?

⌂ How did they affect your beliefs, hopes and aspirations?

⌂ Are there events in your family history that may have affected your genetic development, or the caregiving your received? Do you know how these things affect you?

⌂ What world events, past, current, or future affect you, and how?

⌂ Are you sensitized to threat and disaster?

Picture book page 7: We do not choose our neighbourhood

As with the image of our house, this image portrays westernized homes. Looking beyond that, they represent –

...*city* and *country living*,
prosperity and *deprivation*,
the *demands and pace of life*,
position,
privilege or *disadvantage*,
work and *leisure*,
ambition and *comfort*.

The neighbourhood in which we
grow and live affects our
development,
body and mind,
our *freedom* and *restrictions*,
opportunities, and *limitations*.

It is possible to experience hardship in conditions of wealth or poverty.

 What impact did your neighbourhood have on you?

⌂ What were the conditions in your neighbourhood?

⌂ Did they create ease and comfort, or struggle and difficulty?

⌂ Was your culture and its expression supported and safe?

⌂ Did you and those who raised you experience opportunity or disadvantage?

⌂ Was there adequate opportunity for rest and leisure?

⌂ Was ambition rewarded or undermined?

How did these things affect your life?

Picture book page 8: We do not choose our neighbours

Our neighbours contribute to the environment in which we grow and the world we perceive. Those who live around us can create community in which we feel safe and have a sense of belonging, or we may live with oppression, threat, prejudice, or isolation. Friends and the wider systems with which we interact – school, healthcare, and opportunities for self-expression through hobbies and sports – can support healthy development or inhibit our sense of wellbeing, security, and self-esteem.

What was your neighbourhood like?

⌂ Did you have a sense of safety, wellbeing, possibility or belonging?

⌂ Did you feel accepted and have good, stable friendships?

⌂ Did you experience prejudice or threat?

⌂ Did you have opportunities for success and to build self-esteem?

⌂ Did you have opportunity for hobbies, sports, or other activities for self-expression?

How did your neighbourhood affect you?

Picture book page 9: We do not control how much care we receive

Hardship and difficulties are generally bearable and far less damaging to us when we have support and care from others. The presence of caring others, or enablement, can protect us even in the presence of harm, and can help us to grow and thrive despite difficulty.

Children cannot control the care and attention they receive – this lies within the power and control of adults around them. Whilst it is reasonable to expect that a child's needs will be met by their primary caregivers, many children must "get by" with whatever is on offer. Sometimes they must find other ways in which to meet their needs, physical, psychological, or emotional. It is a resourceful child who finds a way to survive hardship or abuse.

Some children use their imaginations to create the sense of wellbeing they need. Others find ways to convert the attention they receive from others (maybe from a teacher, a health worker, a friend or a beloved pet or animal) into the comfort and love that is otherwise unavailable.

 Who gave you care and support?

⌂ What was the nature of the support you received?

⌂ Was it from another person? Was it practical, emotional, educational, etc?

⌂ How did it support you and what impact did it have on you?

⌂ What affected the care and attention you received?

- How did you find ways to meet your needs?

- Consider what role your imagination and parts may have played in helping you.

- Are you aware that caring and making provision for children is always the responsibility of the adults around them? What effect does that have on you?

Remember that different parts may hold different memories about your care and caregivers.

Try to find ways to accept these differences and to focus on the insights they offer you.

Also consider what needs may have been missed, and how these needs can be met now.

Picture book page 10: We do not choose who raises us

The people we live with have an enormous impact on our lives, our sense of self, our character and our capacity for growth, achievement and satisfaction. With and without our awareness, every aspect of who we are, our personality, our characteristics, our traits, values and dreams, are all positively and negatively affected by those with whom we live and who raise us.

When a child is loved, they learn that they are lovable.

The nature, character, and wellbeing of those who raise us influences how they interact with us, and how we develop. Unresolved, a caregiver's history continues to affect them implicitly and explicitly – physically and practically, in their attitudes, hopes, aspirations, emotions, behaviours and relationship styles. Individuals who experience good and appropriate provision for their childhood needs, love, security, value and purpose, are able to develop internal resources, and are equipped to offer the same to others.

In the absence of healthy support, care and protection, children tend to "pick up" other's problems and personalise them. They form negative beliefs about themselves and think *they* are the source of the problem and to blame. When their needs remain unmet, when they are overlooked – whether through hardship, illness, bereavement, cruelty or ignorance, they may struggle with self-acceptance, self-worth or purpose. They may believe they are "unlovable", "bad", a "nuisance" or that they "don't matter". Once these beliefs are in place, they can act as unidentified but powerful influencers and motivators throughout their lives and may affect future generations in a multitude of ways.

Our experiences with those who raise us, and with whom we live, can create internal conditions of security or of threat. Such effects may or may not be observable. For example, angry caregivers may be unpredictable and frightening. This may provoke alarm and tension in a child who in turn expresses the anger they experience in destructive or bullying behaviours. Conversely, the same angry caregiver may provoke fear or anxiety in a child who learns to live in a state of high alert, unable to relax. This child may seem anxious, unable to concentrate or to make relationships, or they may seem withdrawn or quiet. It's also possible that a child raised by such a caregiver may learn that pleasing adults is crucial to wellbeing, and they may present as perfectly behaved and keen to please. Children's responses are often rationalized or unnoticed until they challenge or cause inconvenience to others around them.

The following questions do not need to be answered fully. They are prompts to help you identify what it was like for you growing up, and what beliefs, helpful or unhelpful, you may have taken on to make life work. The difficulty is that what works when we're young, beliefs or behaviours, may prove unhelpful when we are older. They may be past their "sell-by date"!

What did you learn as you grew?

It is likely that different parts will hold differing, often conflicting memories, beliefs, feelings or goals. Try to accommodate them, to gather insight and to respond with compassion.

⌂ What was your experience of home and/or family?

⌂ How would you describe your relationship with those who raised you?

⌂ Were you able to depend on your caregivers or other adults around you?

⌂ When and with whom did you feel most loved? When and with whom did you feel secure?

⌂ Did you feel important?

⌂ Were your needs reliably met?

⌂ Was it safe to express your needs and emotions?

⌂ Were you listened to? Did you learn that your feelings and opinions mattered?

⌂ Were you encouraged? Did you receive praise, and were you able to bear constructive criticism without it harming your self-esteem?

⌂ How was failure or imperfection viewed?

⌂ How was discipline handled? Did it guide you or crush you?

⌂ Did you learn it was okay to make mistakes?

⌂ What were the "rules" and expectations in your home?

⌂ Were there family secrets or things you were not allowed to talk about?

⌂ How did that affect you?

⌂ Did you have siblings? If so, what was your relationship with them like?

⌂ Were there favourites in your home, and if so, what was that like for you?

⌂ Were you supported in making friends?

⌂ What was your status in relation to your peers?

⌂ Were you able to mix and relate to those around you with confidence?

⌂ What was your experience of illness?

⌂ What was your experience of death?

⌂ Were you healthy? Did you have any disabilities?

⌂ What were your talents? Were they encouraged?

⌂ How would you describe yourself?

⌂ What was your role in your home?

⌂ Did you need to:

　○ Keep the peace?

　○ Make others happy?

　○ Always put others first?

　○ Ignore your feelings?

　○ Keep others at a distance?

　○ Stay busy?

　○ Be helpful?

⌂ How would you complete the following statements?

　○ I am …

　○ I must …

　○ I must not …

- ○ I should …

- ○ I should not …

- ○ I can …

- ○ I can't …

- ○ I like …

- ○ I don't like …

- ○ I deserve …

⌂ What are your greatest longings?

Picture book page 11: *All* parts are trying to help and protect

 Parts may exist with or without our awareness. Parts may also exist without an awareness of one-another or the everyday self. In the picture book "our child" knows there are parts within and introduces us to them here.

When individuals do recognize or accept the presence of parts, they may use that name for them, or may refer to them as "alters" (alternative states), "self-states", "the voices", or other names unique to and reflective of an individual's experience. They may also refer to themselves using plural terms, including "we" or "us". Their presence, and changing states, can make individuals feel disconnected from themselves or the world around them. They may experience unexpected or strong emotions, sensations, pain or a lack of expected sensations, amnesia or "lost time" that is seemingly inexplicable, confusing and/or distressing.

In this image, the parts reflect the ages and stages at which conscious memory was split away, but they also represent the imagined attributes and characteristics needed by our child. When it was preferable to be male or female, older or younger, a particular colour or ethnicity, the parts assumed those presentations. Sometimes parts adopt the characteristics of the abuser to create favour with them, hoping to avoid abuse or to escape the powerlessness they otherwise feel as a victim. Despite mixed presentations and outcomes, and what may seem like conflicting attitudes or tactics, *all parts are trying to help and protect*.

Picture book page 12: a shared body and history

For individuals without parts it can be hard to imagine what it is like to have inner self-states. Individuals with parts often feel similarly, that it is hard to imagine being a "singleton". Singletons can identify conflicting desires and behaviours that undermine their values or goals, but it is difficult for them to understand the inner world or disruption experienced by those with parts with conflicting needs. Common language may mask differences in experience, "… one part of me wants to …" or "my inner critic says …" Most individuals never question or doubt that their inner experience is the same as others.

Parts may remain quiet or hidden, to conceal experiences from the everyday self or others, to establish safety, or to make sure life can carry on with some sense of normality. Parts may also be hidden from one-another, and unaware that they share a body and a life. They may not know that they cannot be seen by external others, nor if the way they believe they look is portrayed in the body's appearance. They may also not recognise time passing, nor know if the body has grown or reached adulthood.

The body stores memories of trauma, and sometimes parts express themselves through the body, through physical health, through sensations, or through a lack of expected sensations or physical control. Memories, or parts, may also be triggered by sensory experiences (touch, smell, taste, sound or sight), or by internal and external sensations, like temperature and pain; survivors or their parts may be phobic of some textures, certain animals or insects, substances or foods or some medical procedures, with or without knowing why.

Picture book page 13: Appearances may be deceiving

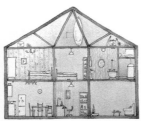

Appearances do not always tell the true, nor the full story … Appearances may be illusory …

It is important we learn to look beyond them, to see what story is being told through a child's behaviour, their attitudes, abilities, characteristics, emotional state, health, capacity for learning and how they cope with setbacks.

Most parents and carers start with good intentions and most births are greeted by positive feelings – even relief. However, if life presses in or caregivers fail to manage, if love loses its way or if adults are intentionally self-seeking and harm children, they have to get by the best way they can – *but* they need other responsible adults who are willing to look past appearances, to take notice, to find ways to support and if necessary, to protect them. Compliance and disruptive behaviour may tell the same story if we listen. They may be fine – or they may not.

It is important to look beyond our prejudices and bias. Wealth, health, status and success, do not mean children are safe from harm, nor do those conditions shield them from it.

Picture book page 14: "... a bad thing happened"

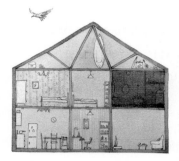

Our child experienced a "bad thing" – and knew it was a bad thing ...

Children use "black and white" thinking. If something seemed bad, or made them feel bad, or sometimes when they are told something is bad or that it was their fault, that is what they will conclude. They are also more likely to believe that they are bad when bad things happen to them, and to avoid telling others for fear of rejection. *But sometimes abuse is confusing ...*

It is natural to feel good when receiving attention, or when someone says, "you're special", or to respond positively to tender touch. We not only want affirming attention, but we also *need* it. However, abusive adults use children for their own satisfaction. They lie to, and manipulate them, so that they can pass on burdens of responsibility or blame to children. They are tricked and pressured into keeping "secrets" and not exposing the adult to judgement or risk.

Children also tend to do as they're told, and to believe what they are told. So, when adults tell them what they should like, or that they made something happen, or that the response of their body proves something – they are unlikely to challenge or to doubt it. Instead, they doubt themselves and mistrust their feelings.

Adults have control – children do not. Our sense of touch is controlled by networks of nerve endings and receptors in our skin. Our response to touch is automatic and outside of our control as can be demonstrated in the knee-jerk reflex. Physical responses are <u>not</u> proof of intention, desire nor enjoyment.

Picture book page 15: Why don't children tell?

Children do as they are told.
Children believe what they are told.

When adults tell them they "cannot tell anyone" – they are likely to believe that. They may be made to feel they were responsible for what happened, told that they "made it happen", or that something bad will happen if they do tell. Sometimes they are threatened with harm to themselves or to others, and sometimes they are simply told they will not be believed.

They may be told that other children experience the same as them, that their experiences are normal and that they should not make a fuss – they have little way of knowing what is true and what is not.

They may have been taught or concluded that something is different about them, or that something is wrong with them, and the shame they feel makes it unlikely they will be able to speak up.

At times they intuitively know that speaking out will cause "trouble" or complications they are unable to face. Sadly, sometimes they accurately assess that "telling" will make things worse or will make no difference. They may be silenced, punished, rejected or mislabelled,[1] and learn to disguise or hide their feelings into adulthood.

Children need to learn about secrets. Good secrets make you feel good inside and include things like lovely presents that have been bought or made for a surprise; bad secrets make you feel bad or confused, jumbled or uncomfortable inside. Children have the right to share bad secrets, and to talk about things that confuse or upset them *with anyone*, no matter what they are told. Grown-ups should never ask nor tell children to keep the bad kinds of secrets.

Children also need to know who they can talk to and when they can do that.
They need to know that what they say will be valued, heard and respected, and that their world can be made better. If they don't know that, how can they tell, and why would they?

Picture book page 16: Dissociation and "splitting"

Dissociative "splitting" or "compartmentalization"[2] may happen when we are unable to integrate experiences into memory. It may also occur as a defensive and protective response to overwhelming threat, situations and/or emotions from which escape is not possible.

When children must endure painful, frightening, or intolerable experiences, or navigate relationships with significant adults or guardians who are sometimes kind but other times cruel – they experience enormous internal conflict. When grown-ups behave unpredictably, severely, or neglectfully, children live with powerlessness and ongoing fear, and need to find ways to manage feelings that could provoke further disruption to the relationships on which they depend. They must suppress or disown "normal" expressions and reactions in favour of responses that keep others happy, and that maintain an illusion of safety, security, or control.

When these experiences are more than is bearable, dissociation and splitting occur spontaneously, and unencoded information and "parts of self" may split away from awareness. Individuals are usually unable to initiate such splitting and remain oblivious to what has happened and to the presence of another part of self. They forget they have forgotten. These parts keep the memories and traumatic experiences separate and beyond deliberate retrieval[3] or recollection. This enables the child to cope and to carry on as normal, which is often essential to safety and wellbeing. The child in our story has become aware of this process and some of her parts and is explaining this to the reader.

When different parts take control of the body, or change places, this is often called "switching"; a discreet change between parts is sometimes called "shifting". Some individuals refer to parts "stepping forward" or "taking control", "being at the front" of simply being "out". Some individuals know when this has happened, by observing loss in time or feelings of detachment and/or disorientation. They describe "waking up in the middle of doing something". Others report being able to observe what is happening, and sometimes without physical sensations, being unable to influence their own behaviour or actions. In other instances, individuals simply have no knowledge of events nor are they aware of discontinuity in time.

When another part has "stepped forward", an individual often presents as usual and commonly attracts no attention – generally an imperative of their existence. However, the protection and support provided by parts can become problematic when individuals are no longer enduring trauma – when parts behave in ways that undermine healthy behaviours or goals, or when the trauma begins to "leak" through amnesic barriers and intrude on everyday life in distressing ways.

The presence of parts may be suspected when significant disruptions are apparent, not exclusively including confusion about identity or a sense of time, forgetting important facts, notable variations in skills and knowledge, substantial fluctuations in emotional states or behaviours, night terrors, phobias or inexplicable physical symptoms. Whilst it is crucial to avoid diagnosing oneself or someone else based on the presence of one or more of these features, their accumulative presence indicate it would be wise to consider and to explore the possibility of dissociation, especially if life has become difficult or even debilitating.

 Do you identify with some of the symptoms mentioned? How many? Would it be helpful take the checklist below to discuss with a professional experienced in dissociative disorders?

☐ Do you have a history of childhood trauma – including significant medical procedures, neglect, and abuse?

☐ Do you feel disconnected from your body or emotions?

☐ Does the world or those around you seem unreal or unfamiliar?

☐ Do you ever feel as though someone else takes control of your body or actions?

⌂ Do you lose time, or have gaps in memory for large chunks of time or important events?

⌂ Do you experience confusion or conflict about who you are?

⌂ Are you "changeable", or do you experience significant swings of emotion?

⌂ Do you experience varying abilities and skills, sometimes you can – sometimes you can't?

⌂ Do you present significantly differently, in attitudes, behaviours, voice or language?

⌂ Do you ever discover that you own things you have no memory of buying?

⌂ Do people ever greet you by another name, but you have no idea who they are?

⌂ Do you have nightmares or intrusive images with frightening content?

⌂ Do you have unexpected intense swells of emotion, that bear no relation to current time?

⌂ Do you experience unprovoked pain, sensations, or a lack of expected physical sensations?

⌂ Do you hear voices or thoughts that do not seem like your own?[4]

⌂ Do you have phobias?

⌂ Do you experience significant distress or disruption caused by any items noted above?

⌂ Are the effects experienced unexplainable – not occurring in relation to drug use or alcohol nor attributable to another disorder?

Picture book page 17: When "bad" keeps happening

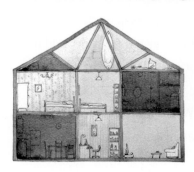

Ongoing trauma is referred to as "complex" or "chronic" trauma; it is usually interpersonal and has a strong relationship[5] with dissociation and dissociative disorders.

In our picture book, traumatic experiences are portrayed as "bad things" that happen, as events. However, trauma and resulting dissociation may occur when neglect or a lack of care and provision creates severe or hostile environments.[6]

Acute neglect can be difficult to measure, and emotional and psychological abuse may be hard to prove. The evidence is found in the symptoms they create and the legacies they leave behind. "Small t" traumas, so-called because they often remain unnoticed or can be minimised, are cumulative, and have significant impacts and effects.

Picture book page 18: Dissociation is generally spontaneous

When trauma or abuse occurs and continues, it disrupts the ways in which memory is stored and accessed, and under great duress, different parts of self may split away or simply remain unintegrated and fragmented. The ability to dissociate occurs involuntarily, but thereafter may continue to happen spontaneously in response to trauma, trauma triggers and reminders.[7]

Multiple parts may emerge from one event as the traumatised child tries to adapt to the situation and demands. The "sequential model"[8] of dissociation proposes that the child may fragment according to different roles they must adopt to cope. For example, when confronted by threat, they may become passive or quiet to avoid being noticed. If that is unsuccessful, they may adopt an aggressive or fearless stance to try to discourage approach, or they may inwardly collapse and accept mistreatment. Parts may reflect the trauma response, or the need to maintain normal appearances in order to minimise ongoing risk.

In the images on pages 18 and 19, our child is portrayed in different situations, some play, but mostly portraying an image of being "okay". When trauma is unresolved or abuse is ongoing, parts maintain a sense of normalcy to create some sense of safety; they may even ensure survival.

Picture book page 19: Maintaining normal ...

Switching may occur unnoticed – by other people, by the everyday self or even by parts. Subtle changes between parts are often called "shifting".

When individuals are unaware of their parts, they may simply believe they are extremely changeable, emotional, or unpredictable. When they are unaware of parts *and* switches, they may have no awareness or memory of events or their behaviours; they may feel disconcerted by others' reports about their actions. Even when individuals do recognise the existence of other parts and switching, it is often in their interests to mask this process, to avoid drawing attention to themselves, an experience that may previously have made them vulnerable.

Sometimes "distance" is deliberately reinforced by the everyday self and parts to ensure emotion and memory is not shared between them. In particular, the everyday self may have limited tolerance or ability to handle such affects and may even experience a phobic degree of avoidance.

In this image, we see some of our child's parts, distinctive and divided from one-another. We can see their different responses – reaching out for connection, getting away, confused, frustrated, deep in thought and avoiding, each doing what they can to help.

Picture book page 20: Who will come?

Parts may reflect the age and gender of the child under duress. However, our minds are resourceful and often intuitively characterise parts according to need and demand. This means parts may reflect the characteristics or skills apparently needed.

An older child may be perceived as having the composure or abilities required to respond more appropriately to the situation, or a younger child may seemingly represent needed characteristics – sweetness, compliance, or innocence; a boy might be needed for a manifestation of strength or to avoid accepting a felt sense of weakness; a girl might be needed to manage sexual advances or to respond with sensitivity. The parts may reflect attributes of their abuser, to enable them to cope with aversion or conflict, or to create an acceptable impression of affiliation or connection.

The everyday self, and parts, may be unable to influence these responses and who shows up! It can be disorienting and distressing, and parts may be confused and feel themselves at odds with one another.

Picture book page 21: When the body belongs to us all

The picture book, and this image, portrays *one* everyday self, accompanied by many other parts. Some survivors have *many* everyday selves, who help manage varying responsibilities and roles in daily life; others may have only one everyday self and one part. The everyday self/selves represent part of the whole unintegrated individual and may also be considered parts. More is written about this in Chapter 2: Dissociation – a continuum.

Parts play an important role in a survivor's life and some may develop a strong sense of self, individuality, and history. These parts may select a name that is unique to them and different from the everyday self. If it is important that their presence is concealed, they may remain hidden, even from one-another and might not realise they share the same body nor the same life. Furthermore, their strategies for defense or for coping can vary widely. This creates poor conditions for co-operation, and even when aware of one-another, the everyday self or their parts may remain suspicious of one-another or hostile and resistant to the strategies and behaviours adopted by others.

Taking care of the body can be a challenge for some who have mistreated it in an attempt to make sense of pain or distress, or who have used it to act out risky behaviours in an attempt to resolve past victimization. Others may have disdain for the imagined weakness of the body or despise it because it represents everything bad that happened. Learning to care for the body may be hard, but ultimately helps survivors to leave the trauma behind. Accepting that each part emerged to shield or defend against threat is often a helpful starting point when learning about each part, their roles and their potential, and respect fosters possibility for collaboration and resolution of traumatic symptoms.

Picture book page 22: Whose choice?

Everyday selves or parts may "come to the front" and take charge of the body and life, with or without the knowledge or the awareness of other parts.

Parts may be able to observe events, or to share memory of experiences between themselves. This is often referred to as "co-consciousness". However, even when co-consciousness exists, it does not necessarily include every part. Without it, individuals experience a disruption in continuity and memory, which is often described as "losing time".

Time loss can be very disruptive, accounting for seconds, hours or much longer and individuals may lack important information or control for daily challenges. It may pass unnoticed since it's hard to remember when you don't know that you forgot, or it may be so commonplace for a survivor that they fail to question whether or not others have the same experience. Conversely, they may feel uncomfortable about their own forgetfulness and try to conceal it.

"Not knowing" can be helpful when life is more than we can bear. However, when threat and danger are past, the lack of ongoing memory can prevent individuals from reclaiming their lives and healing the hurt they experienced; it can also make them vulnerable to risk from perpetrators.

Picture book page 23: Co-conscious, co-present

Dissociation does not create a solid memory barrier. Survivors may experience unexpected and/or distressing sensations, images and feelings as flashbacks or "leaks" from memory, often without context.

The everyday self/selves have generally been able to manage life because they have been shielded from memory and overwhelming feelings. They may want that to continue and to avoid remembering the past or experiences that can still provoke strong responses.

Some parts may be hostile to the everyday self/selves, whom they believe abandoned them, or whom they perceive as weak. Other parts, especially younger ones, have needs for comfort and connection that some may struggle to acknowledge or to meet. This can foster ongoing separation and rejection between selves/parts. Even so, remaining separate and unaware of different parts causes disruptions to everyday life, and may even make individuals vulnerable to risk.

"Co-consciousness" is when selves have an awareness of one-another or of the internal "system". When there is greater co-consciousness, the everyday self or parts may be able to observe the actions of others. It may also enable parts to share knowledge of experiences, to share memory, and/or varying degrees of control over the body, so that time loss and subsequent disruption is minimised. In some instances, it enables "co-presence", when parts may share experiences and control of the body at the same time.

However, parts do not naturally trust one-another, and co-consciousness may exist between some parts and exclude others. Communication and connection need to be accompanied by mutual respect and empathy. When this is nurtured, co-consciousness can help create internal co-operation, less fragmentation, greater safety and make life work more smoothly.

Picture book page 24: Who is in charge?

Parts, including the everyday self or selves, may be unable to choose who is present and in charge of the body – "at the front" – at any given stage. Some may be triggered by reminders of past trauma, and find themselves in charge, and needing to cope with risks, perceived or real. However, responses that were helpful when young and facing significant threat, can be unhelpful or inappropriate when that threat has passed. Whilst parts initially offered protection, their strategies are sometimes out-dated or maladaptive for life as an adult with greater autonomy or choice.

When parts *are* able to influence who is in charge, they may feel frustrated that they need to give greater time and control to the everyday self in order to conceal themselves. They may subsequently push forwards and take control whenever it seems safer to do so, or when they choose, without collaboration with others inside. With different talents, abilities, and attitudes, changes in control may also produce a varying skillset that can be very difficult to manage. Clients report being able to do things, or to remember things, "sometimes". It makes sense therefore, that a lack of awareness of parts, influence over them or collaboration, can be frustrating and confusing.

Picture book page 25: When parts do what they know best

Responses to trauma are triggered automatically by the body's survival mechanisms – biologically in-built for protection.

When danger is detected, instinctive reactions mobilise to protect against threat. When threat is perceived our brain releases cortisol and adrenaline to increase heart and respiratory rate and blood pressure, and our muscle tone increases to ready us for a response, to fight (defend or attack), for flight (escape) or freeze (shut down).

When these responses are inhibited or blocked, or when trauma remains unresolved, individuals can stay in a state of high alert, sensitive to danger or reminders of their experience. Such experiences can also affect the body's reactivity to danger, making it more easily triggered thereafter. Even when triggers are unobserved consciously, they may activate a stress response, and an individual may be flooded with strong emotions, sensations, or images as if events are occurring currently. Repetition reinforces the activation of these responses until they become automatic and parts that split away in response to threat may subsequently assume roles that mirror these protective tasks, including:

Fight
When possible, forceful, or dominant action may defend the body and the mind. Powerful hormones energise and increase physical strength to fight off an attacker or perceived threat. However, when activated outside

of trauma time, this response and parts who have taken on this role, continue to behave in similar ways, with strong responses designed to protect. These parts may express themselves aggressively, angrily, or in hostile or destructive ways. They tend to be mistrusting or hostile and can be impulsive. They also tend to take control, and will consider self-destructive responses, including suicidality, rather than submit to being overpowered by others or by circumstance.

Flight

When fight is not possible – for example if the threat or power of an attacker is greater than the strength possessed, the next option is for flight – "can we run and get away from danger?" When this response is reactivated, an individual or parts with this role feel all the previous intensity of the desire to escape and to create distance from threat, which may include emotional or sensory replay. In order to achieve this, these parts may distance themselves from others or sabotage relationships. They may also use substances, drugs or alcohol to escape feelings, or employ strategies including depersonalisation and derealisation to distance themselves from current time. In this state, the everyday self/selves and/or parts may describe feeling "spacey" or "disconnected".

Freeze

This response occurs when the threat is immense and when options of escape or fight are impossible or unlikely to be successful. The higher reasoning parts of the brain shut down and the body becomes numb or paralysed in a survival response that is designed to thwart detection or to protect against pain. Post trauma time, this response remains equally sensitive to reactivation. Individuals and parts who hold these responses experience a flooding of emotion, often setting off internal alarm responses that activate other parts and reactions. In everyday life, they are terrified of being noticed or of receiving attention, and often experience hypersensitivity to fear or anxiety that can also manifest in phobias or panic attacks.

Submit

 When fight and flight are impossible, submission can minimise aggression or violence. These parts often endured abuse when others could not. With hindsight, they may misperceive their compliance as willingness and carry shame that should belong to the abuser. This is reinforced by perpetrators, who tell children they are willing participants, or that automatic physical responses indicate desire.

When these memories or feelings are reactivated, an individual and these parts may respond similarly to trauma time, conforming to others' wishes and being passive. They can also respond to others' requests or demands without consideration of their own needs. However, they carry a burden of shame and self-hatred that often translates into significant depression and an ongoing felt sense of hopelessness and powerlessness.

Attach

 Once again, when fight and flight are not achievable, an attach response is intended to provoke a favourable reaction in others, to promote connection that will provoke care or nurture. It often originates in abuse experienced by young children and parts who need and long for healthy connection, or for rescue or help.

When activated post trauma time, an individual and these parts experience desperate yearnings for relationship, for protection, rescue, and safety. These parts are often quite young and longing to be loved. Driven by strong felt need and insecure attachment, their behaviours and strategies may at times manifest as dependence. Their instinctive desires may compel them to maintain abusive relationships with significant others, with a childlike hope that they will one day achieve good relationship and have their needs met in healthy ways.

<<>>

The everyday self may be pushed back whilst parts take over to protect in the way they know best. The everyday self may be unaware of events or they may become an observer with little influence over them; they may feel equally overwhelmed and out of control as they lack the opportunity for resolution or to develop new skills and resilience. Subsequently, their ability to manage life may become compromised or restricted.

Parts can remain at odds with one another since their roles and strategies are often contradictory and may seem to engender risk. A significant challenge for parts and the everyday self/selves is recognising that each strategy adopted was designed for protection. Additionally, whilst these responses would have been adaptive in childhood, they can be particularly inhibitory in adulthood. Parts who continue to live in "trauma time", or who remain sensitised to danger, may be unable to recognise the resources available to an adult self, or unwilling to relinquish control in case of failure.

Picture book page 26: When others don't understand

If only it was feasible to calmly consider the demands of situations and then to make reasonable and adaptive responses – but it's just not that easy! Sometimes, it's not even possible …

When young, the everyday self and parts would have learned to adjust their behaviours according to demands, to their situation and their interpretation of it. They may have managed this well, or sometimes inappropriately. They may have been, and may remain, confusing to themselves as well as to others.

When triggered, making a distinction between past and current threat is enormously difficult. Without internal awareness, healing and collaboration, parts will continue to behave as if threat is still present. They may or may not know what triggered them and will tend to respond first and reflect second – a response that may have kept them alive previously.

When looking through the lens of trauma, with insight and appreciation of their experience, their behaviours make perfect sense. A trauma-informed society and care providers need to learn to ask, "what has happened to this person?" rather than "what is wrong with this person?" Understanding and compassion can begin within, as individuals search for support and help that is based on awareness, respect, collaboration and empowerment.

Picture book page 27: I don't want you!

The everyday self often struggles with the emotions and reactions they attribute to their parts. They can be rejecting of them and may wish they would simply "go away". In some circumstances they may value the presence and support of certain parts and the jobs they fulfil, whilst feeling resentful or frustrated with others.

As in the external world and in regular relationships, some parts have a natural empathy for, or understanding of one-another, whilst others prefer to avoid those with whom they believe they have little in common or who inhibit their ambitions. As noted in the comments for page 25, the strategies and aims of different parts can be conflicting and create mistrust or hostility between them. The parts who protect through fight or aggressive responses find the attachment aims and submissive behaviours of others dangerous and triggering. They may feel angry and frustrated by the tender desires and actions of those parts. Those whose role has been to submit and to search for connections find that their goals are blocked or undermined by parts whose job it is to fight or escape as they push away or withdraw from relationships. These relational parts are unable to meet their needs and remain isolated and in pain.

Validating the different needs, roles and aims of each part can help them learn to appreciate and support one-another – ultimately creating the conditions needed for recovery and empowering all parts for growth and healthy change.

Picture book page 28: Help and cooperation

The everyday self/selves and parts share the same body.
They share the same life.
They share the same history.
They share a future ...

"We" is a state of shared belonging and responsibility. For recovery and healing, everyone will need to learn how to cooperate and to foster respect between one-another. Aims and goals will need to be negotiated.

Recovery starts with safety and self-care. Some parts may need to work on memories to achieve safety, whilst others may find that making sense of their experiences and the creation of stability provides sufficient wellbeing. Each part will need respect and opportunity to create the resolution that is right for them, whilst also courageously making compromises for other's welfare.

Compromise is likely to have been a frightening feature of many traumatic experiences when the choice was between something bad or something terrible. Each insider will need empathy and sensitivity to learn that it can serve security, health, and happiness. Support and help from friends and professionals who understand helps sustain survivors in recovery and is important when learning how to trust.

Picture book page 29: When living together is tricky!

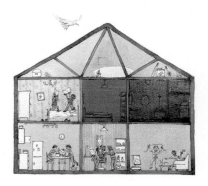

Having DID or parts is not an illness that needs curing, nor can parts just disappear. They may be silent or hidden, but without help, they remain within, holding trauma memory separate, and still in need of comfort and help.

Sensitivity to triggers and internal conflict can make life difficult for every part. Self-compassion for every "self" is required for internal harmony and recovery – but it can be scary for a trauma survivor. It can feel like they are setting themselves up for a fall, for hope that will only be destroyed, or for weakness that will make them vulnerable. However, compassion can build strength, unity and resourcefulness. Learning about each part and creating mutual respect and appreciation, helps survivors to create greater safety as well as creating congruence and inner peace.

Some survivors and their parts work with a therapist to resolve the legacies of trauma. They are supported as they find out about one-another and develop self-insight; they learn how to bring their abilities and skills to the fore, and once again discover how to adapt – but this time for safety. Parts may process and integrate traumatic experiences, so that the past no longer has the power to influence them. They can also learn how to avoid retraumatising one-another and how to encourage and protect rather than criticise or self-sabotage.

Sometimes parts take on new roles that serve current life, ambitions, and welfare in better ways; sometimes they choose to blend with one-another, (also called fusion or integration), creating a new experience and expression of self. These choices are very individual, and all parts will need support to negotiate choices and preferences.

Picture book page 30: Learning about trust, and *then* learning to trust

Trust is broken by interpersonal trauma; it is repaired in relationship. Finding someone to trust is frightening but crucial to recovery, but what makes someone trustworthy?

How do *you* identify a safe person?
How many of the safe traits below would they need to demonstrate to make them a good risk?
How many of the unsafe traits would make them unsafe for you? Are some traits more important than others?

Safe people:

⌂ Accept you as you are

⌂ Are interested in your feelings and what matters to you

⌂ Accept and encourage your right to boundaries and limits

⌂ Listen without judgement, and take you seriously

⌂ Accept your "yes" or "no" without scolding

⌂ Tell you the truth *with* kindness

⌂ Give you the right to change your mind

⌂ Are forgiving

○ Encourage you to share your opinions and beliefs without criticism

○ Are open to feedback without risk of reprisal

○ Admit their weaknesses

○ Take responsibility for their own mistakes

○ Apologise *and* make efforts to avoid making the same errors

○ Take care of themselves

○ Encourage you to reach your potential

When it is difficult to identify safe traits, it is sometimes easier to look for characteristics that make someone unsafe:

Unsafe people:

○ Are proud and demanding

○ Do not accept your boundaries or limitations

○ Criticise or put you down

○ Make fun of you or others

○ Refuse to accept your rights to choose, your "yes" or "no"

○ Trick or lie to you

○ Hurt you

○ Refuse to acknowledge their mistakes, and tend to blame others

○ Apologize *without changing* their behaviours

○ Are defensive or hostile

○ Are aggressive, controlling, or violent

○ Are unforgiving

○ Expect others to take care of them

Do you agree? What would you add?

Picture book page 31: We all deserve to be okay ...

Healing from trauma and dissociation *is* possible – including complex trauma and chronic childhood abuse.

Creating conditions of safety and respect enables internal co-operation and allows each part to receive the care and support they need to recover. When traumatic experience is processed, and integrated into our minds and histories, parts can jointly decide how to take life forward.

They will need time to adjust to changes, as well as time and support to consider helpful and purposeful ways to use their skills and talents. Some parts may choose to create healthier internal conditions so that they can relax and enjoy the inner world. Some who long for attachment, may help foster healthy and trusting relationships; parts who helped with fight or flight responses may help establish safety, determining who is worthy of trust and learning how to calm the body in positive ways. Co-operation between parts can create harmony and contribute towards wellbeing.

When traumatic experiences are resolved, some parts may choose to "blend" or "fuse", leaving fragmentation behind and embracing greater unity and a sense of wholeness. Collaboration and understanding *between parts* are important when making these choices, which are very personal. No part, nor individual should feel pressured to make a choice for blending or fusion, nor for remaining separate.

Adjusting to life, with or without internal companions and without dissociative responses, is likely to be part of the journey of healing and growth. Whatever is decided, living free from fear and dysregulation, and with greater peace of mind, releases energy that can be redirected towards living well.

Picture book page 32: We all have an inner child

If you are reading, or being read the words in this book, you may have an awareness of your inner child, of the "little you" that came before you ...

You may not have become the person you wanted to be ...
You may need to find your younger self, to rescue that younger you from fears or losses, and to help bind up wounds while they heal.
You may find surprising joys, or hopes that your younger self has held.

You are likely to find that your younger self was resilient, resourceful and strong – and deserves your respect, nurture and support.

It may be time to reclaim the life you longed for – to be the person you could have been or the person you wanted to be.[9]

Restoring your inner world, reclaiming what was taken from you, and recovering your inner child or parts, may take time, compassion, courage, and patience. Refuse to be defined by the treatment you received or the unhealthy or cruel people who hurt you. If you can, find some journey companions who will help encourage you when you're weary, draw alongside you in your pain, guide you when you feel lost, stay strong when you feel weak and stay steady when you feel afraid. If you are still struggling to find people who will help you in that way – please take on my hope, my confidence, that you can.

Notes

1   Appropriate learning and screening tools help distinguish the differences between dissociative disorders, powerful imagination, and psychosis.

2   Somer, E., 2011. Dissociation in traumatized children and adolescents, in V. Ardino (ed.), *Post-traumatic syndromes in childhood and adolescence*. Wiley-Blackwell. doi:10.1002/9780470669280.ch8.

3   Professor Chris Brewin and colleagues conduct research into the accuracy and/or limitations of memory. They have regularly concluded that whilst memory may be malleable, it is *not* unreliable. Brewin, C.R., Andrews, B. & Mickes, L., 2020. Regaining consensus on the reliability of memory. *Current Directions in Psychological Science*, 29(2), pp. 121–125.

4   Distinct from auditory hallucinations in psychosis. Please see note in the Chapter 2: Dissociation: a continuum, p. XX, and endnote 21.

5   Putnam, F.W., 1985. Dissociation as a response to extreme trauma, in R.P. Kluft (Ed.), *Childhood antecedents of multiple personality*, pp. 63–97. Washington, DC: American Psychiatric Press.

6   West, M., Adam, K., Spreng, S. & Rose. S., 2001. Attachment disorganization and dissociative symptoms in clinically treated adolescents. *Canadian Journal of Psychiatry*, 46(7), pp. 627–631.

7   Please see Chapter 2: Dissociation – a continuum for more information.

8   Also well described in Danylchuk, L. & Connors, K., 2016. *Treating complex trauma and dissociation: A practical guide to navigating therapeutic challenges*, pp. 24–25.

9   "The type of person you wish you were is who you really are, but haven't yet learnt to be", Penny Parks, originator of Parks Inner Child Therapy, PICT.

7 Additional resources

This chapter offers recommendations to sources of information and support, some that have proven reliable and helpful to the author, and some that have been recommended by other practitioners and/or survivors. The list is neither exhaustive nor all-inclusive but offered in the hope readers will find them helpful and at least a good starting point. Some are specific to survivors and their caregivers, some to practitioners, but it is anticipated that valuable information and insights may be found in all.

Please note: In this evolving field new material is continually being developed. Recommendations cannot ensure reliability, nor the appropriateness of material to any individual or their parts. When engaging with any site or material, wisdom and care are necessary to ensure learning is paced, and if an individual has parts, with consideration for their needs and capacities.

Self-help books (listed alphabetically)

+ *Becoming Safely Embodied, A Guide to Organize Your Mind, Body and Heart to Feel Secure in the World*, (2021) by Deirdre Fay. A model that provides step-by-step skills training for safe living within one's own skin, for staying present, and for sorting emotions and sensations

+ *Coping with Trauma-Related Dissociation: Skills Training for Patients and Therapists*, (2011) by Suzette Boon, Kathy Steele and Onno van der Hart. Whilst recommended for use alongside therapeutic support, this outstanding book is comprehensive in breadth and depth; it is well organised and accessible to both novice and experienced survivors and practitioners

+ *Dear Little Ones*, (2015+) by Jade Miller, is a trilogy of books written by a survivor of ritualised abuse, to help her own young parts. The first book helps younger parts understand they have value and belonging, and how things have changed over time; the second book talks about healing from hurtful parental relationships and learning to love oneself; the third encourages parts to work out what wholeness might look like according to their own choices

+ *Got Parts? An Insider's Guide to Managing Life Successfully with Dissociative Identity Disorder*, (2005) by ATW. A practical guide to managing life successfully with DID, including coping strategies for everyday living and ideas for real-life issues – relationships, work, parenting, school, time, self-care and medical treatment

+ *Healing Trauma*, (2008) by Peter Levine. Recommended in "book with CD" format. This material includes guided exercises to help individuals develop body awareness and to resolve and clear the effects of trauma stored in the body. It also includes emergency "first aid" measures for responding to distress and discovering the physiological roots of emotions. Dr Levine is the originator of Somatic

DOI: 10.4324/9781003148128-8

Experiencing, a body-oriented approach to healing trauma and stress disorders (https://traumahealing
.org/)

➕ *It's Not You, It's What Happened to You: Complex Trauma and Treatment*, (2020) by Christine Courtois.
Primarily written for those new to the subject, this book provides a thorough and easy-to-read
explanation of complex trauma, how it develops and manifests and how to manage it

➕ *It's Not Me: Understanding Complex Trauma, Attachment and Dissociation*, (2018) by Anabel Gonzalez.
A compassionate, engaging and informative book aimed at patients and family members of complex
trauma survivors

➕ *Transforming the Living Legacy of Trauma: A Workbook for Survivors and Therapists*, (2021) by Janina
Fisher. This exceptional book gives information about symptoms and reactions to traumatic experiences,
normalising and validating them. It offers step-by step strategies that may be used individually or in
collaboration with a practitioner, to help survivors navigate and recover from the legacies of trauma

Specialist self-help book

➕ *Becoming Yourself: Overcoming Mind Control and Ritual Abuse*, (2014) by Alison Miller. This unique,
jargon-free book was developed for survivors of organised and ritualised abuse. It informs and equips
survivors and offers information about resulting complex personality systems and symptoms. It gives
practical advice for achieving stability, safety, and internal cooperation, and as each part's needs are
met, for resolving traumatic memories and conditioning

Survivor-recommended theoretical books

➕ *Healing the Fragmented Selves of Trauma Survivors: Overcoming Internal Self-Alienation*, (2017) by
Janina Fisher. Hailed by experts, this book synthesises a neurobiological understanding of attachment,
trauma and dissociation with a practical, compassionate and thorough approach to treatment.
Interventions are adapted from neuroscience, Sensorimotor Psychotherapy, Internal Family Systems, and
mindfulness and sensitively focus on key issues of shame, self-loathing and guilt

➕ *The Body Keeps the Score: Mind, Brain and Body in the Transformation of Trauma*, (2015) by Bessel van
der Kolk. This exceptional book explains how overwhelming experiences affect the development of mind,
body and awareness. Integrating clinical case examples, neuroscience, and a deep understanding of the
pain and devastation survivors experience, it also introduces innovative treatments that offer genuine
hope for recovery

+ *Trauma and Recovery*, (2015) by Judith Herman. This seminal "go-to" text focuses on the effects and symptoms of trauma and elaborates the now leading staged approach to recovery. It is informative and thorough whilst maintaining an empathetic tone. It highlights the connection between mental health and social and political contexts to empower and give voice to survivors and professionals committed to recovery

Treatment guidelines

Adults

+ ISSTD Adult Treatment Guidelines: www.isst-d.org/resources/adult-treatment-guidelines/

+ BLUE KNOT Practice Guidelines: www.blueknot.org.au/resources/Publications/Practice-Guidelines

+ BLUE KNOT Supervision Guidelines: www.blueknot.org.au/Resources/Publications/Practice-Guidelines/Supervision-Guidelines

Children

+ ISSTD Child Adolescent Treatment Guidelines: www.isst-d.org/resources/child-adolescent-treatment-guidelines/

+ ESTD More Resources: https://estduk.org/resources/

Online sites (listed alphabetically)

Please note it is not possible to vouch for evolving content, so personal judgement and discrimination needs to be exercised when visiting any site. If visiting chat sites and communities, it is also important to be aware that not all visitors to such sites are safe.

+ An Infinite Mind: www.aninfinitemind.com/about.html

   A non-profit organisation dedicated to improving the lives of people living with trauma-based dissociation, primarily focused on Dissociative Identities. AIM provides information and seeks to develop awareness and understanding about DID through trainings, engaging with the media, delivering workshops, and holding an annual conference for survivors, their loved ones, and professionals

+ Blue Knot Foundation: www.blueknot.org.au/

   BKF is a national Australian organisation which "empowers recovery and builds resilience for adults impacted by complex trauma". An outstanding site for its quality and breadth of content, it provides information and support to survivors and their supporters. It also provides training and resources to build professional knowledge, skill and trauma-informed communities

🔸 Carolyn Spring: www.carolynspring.com/

Carolyn is a survivor, author and a speaker who combines a rich depth of learning and lived experience to make these complex subjects accessible to all. *Carolyn's site* offers helpful information and training opportunities relevant to survivors and professionals, including an excellent "Emotional Resource Guide", 2016

🔸 ESTD – European Society for Trauma and Dissociation: www.estd.org/

A European organisation committed to increasing understanding of trauma, dissociation, related conditions, and their treatment. The ESTD promotes clinical collaboration and research and provides education and training, as well as links to other organisations and sites: www.estd.org/board/links

ESTD-UK has excellent links to free resources for professionals and individuals, including information for working with children and adolescents: https://estduk.org/resources/

🔸 ESTSS – European Society for Traumatic Stress Studies: https://estss.org/

Based in the Netherlands, ESTSS supports professionals by promoting "the sharing of knowledge and experience about all aspects of psychotraumatology ... by fostering research and best practice, building networks and by contribution to public policy at a European level"

🔸 FPP – First Person Plural: www.firstpersonplural.org.uk/

A charity that specialises in working for and on behalf of those affected by DID and similar complex trauma-related dissociative conditions. They aim to improve knowledge, understanding and recognition of these conditions, to encourage and facilitate support, and to improve access to specialist assessment and effective care and treatment

🔸 Healing from Complex Trauma and PTSD/CPTSD: www.healingfromcomplextraumaandptsd.com/

An award-winning site created by Lilly Hope Lucario, written from the perspective of a survivor. It aims to empower, support, and inform individuals and caregivers journeying through healing, and also offers rich insights to professionals

🔸 ISSTD – International Society for the Study of Trauma and Dissociation: https://www.isst-d.org/

An international non-profit professional association promoting "comprehensive, clinically effective and empirically based resources and responses to trauma and dissociation, and to address its relevance to other theoretical constructs". Although funded through membership, the site provides good non-member resources, including treatment guidelines, screening and assessment tools, training opportunities and public resources, including fact sheets and links to websites of interest

🔸 ISTSS – International Society for Traumatic Stress Studies: https://istss.org/home

An international Society "dedicated to sharing information about the effects of trauma and the discovery and dissemination of knowledge about policy, program and service initiatives that seek to reduce traumatic stressors and their immediate and long-term consequences". Provides information for professionals and education materials for the public

+ Ivory Garden: https://igdid.org/

    A non-profit online organisation that provides support to survivors and their supporters. It also aims to raise awareness about the effects of childhood trauma through the provision of educational resources and opportunities and hosts international forums and chat rooms where individuals can meet, share, and provide respectful support to one-another

+ Sidran Institute: https://www.sidran.org/

    A non-profit international organisation offering information, education and hope to individuals and professionals engaging in treatment and recovery from traumatic stress, dissociative disorders and co-occurring problems such as self-injury, addiction and suicidality. The site offers training and resources to survivors and their loved ones, helpers, professionals and the media, as well as links to other resources: https://www.sidran.org/links-to-other-trauma-resources/

Videos

+ *A Logical Way of Being* – this film introduces DID and other complex dissociative conditions. It gives information about their primary features and some understanding about their origins. Viewers also gain insight into what it is like to live with DID and are presented with information about the support needs of individuals as well as the role of psychotherapeutic treatment

+ *No Two Paths the Same* – is an educative film that explains and offers insights into a phase-oriented treatment approach for DID. It presents information on each phase (stabilisation, processing and consolidation) and includes supportive information for partners of people with DID

    Both of the videos listed above are available as a DVD or as an MP4 from First Person Plural: www.firstpersonplural.org.uk/resources/training-films/

+ *May 33rd* – a film by Guy Hibbert, explores the consequences of chronic ritual abuse, as seen through the eyes of Ella whose personality has fragmented into five different people. This film is difficult to source. Under restricted license conditions, it is available to members of the ESTD-UK for professional training and CPD purposes

Treatment books (a few suggestions, listed alphabetically)

+ *Rebuilding Shattered Lives, Treating Complex PTSD and Dissociative Disorders,* 2nd ed, (2011) by James Chu. A valuable book for beginners and experienced clinicians, this text offers practical advice on therapeutic techniques and treatment, with information about early attachments and their effects, neurobiology, crisis management and psychopharmacology

⚜ *Shelter from the Storm: Processing the Traumatic Memories of DID/DDNOS Patients with the Fractionated Abreaction Technique,* (2013) by Richard Kluft. Integrates elements from psychoanalysis, psychodynamic psychotherapy, hypnosis, behavioural therapy, cognitive therapy, and EMDR to support a practical, empathic, and compassionate approach to treatment, taking care to avoid retraumatisation

⚜ *The Haunted Self: Structural Dissociation and the Treatment of Chronic Traumatisation,* (2006) by Onno van der Hart, Ellert Nijenhuis and Kathy Steele. This key text draws attention to the substantial problems suffered by chronically traumatised individuals. It presents the theory of structural dissociation of the personality, a phase-oriented approach to treatment, and hope that recovery is achievable

⚜ *Trauma Model Therapy: A Treatment Approach for Trauma Dissociation and Complex Comorbidity,* (2009) by Colin Ross. A practical, well-structured manual, comprehensively presenting theory, assessment and treatment strategies, techniques and interventions for severe dissociative disorders

⚜ *Treating Complex Trauma and Dissociation – a practical guide to navigating therapeutic challenges,* (2017) by Lynette Danylchuk and Kevin Connors. This highly readable book combines clinical experience and insight. It presents clear and practical information to support understanding and offers guidance for navigating a phased approach to treatment, handling foundational issues and potential challenges

⚜ *Treating Trauma-Related Dissociation: A Practical, Integrative Approach,* (2017) by Kathy Steele, Suzette Boon and Onno van der Hart. Written by leading experts, this comprehensive text extends the content of the skills training manual, (listed in the "Self-Help" section). It offers a practical, thorough, and insightful approach to treatment based on the structural dissociation model

⚜ *Treatment of Dissociative Identity Disorder: Techniques and Strategies for Stabilisation,* (2018) by Colin Ross. Practical, concise and informative, especially useful for practitioners new to working with DID

⚜ *Working with Voices and Dissociative Parts – A Trauma-informed approach,* (2nd edn, 2019) by Dolores Mosquera. A comprehensive, elaborative, and inspirational workbook, that is truly integrative, structured, collaborative, and informative for both the novice and the senior practitioner

Specialist information and sources

Working with children and adolescents (books listed alphabetically)

⚜ *Child/adolescent treatment guidelines,* www.isst-d.org/resources/child-adolescent-treatment-guidelines/ Updated recommendations for the assessment and treatment of children and adolescents with symptoms of dissociation are available on the ESTD site: www.estd.org/treatment-guidelines

+ *Dissociation in Traumatized Children and Adolescents: Theory and Clinical Interventions, 2nd edn*, (2015) by Sandra Wieland. Presents compelling case studies that elaborate the variability of dissociation in children and adolescents, and practical insights into five models of dissociation to support understanding and the application of therapeutic guidelines and interventions

+ *Healing the Fractured Child: Diagnosis & Treatment of Youth with Dissociation*, (2015) by Frances S. Waters. Provides a wealth of information to support understanding, assessment, and creative treatment strategies and interventions for working with children, adolescents and families recovering from traumatic experiences

+ *Nurturing Children: From Trauma to Growth Using Attachment Theory, Psychoanalysis and Neurobiology*, (2019) by Graham Music. Distils and clarifies the interactions between mind and body, and the role of attachment as a source of trauma and recovery. Includes authentic reflections from the heart and mind of a highly respected practitioner

+ *The Child Survivor: Healing Developmental Trauma and Dissociation*, 2nd edn, (2021) by Joyanna Silberg. A widely respected, comprehensive, and practical resource for treating children and adolescents with dissociative symptoms. Including information on assessment and treatment, and case examples to illustrate clinical dilemmas, this book has been praised by practitioners and adult survivors

+ *The Simple Guide to Complex Trauma and Dissociation: What It Is and How to Help*, (2020) by Betsy de Thierry. Written to complement *The Simple Guide to Child Trauma*, this book takes complex theories and clarifies them, to inform and offer practical advice to individuals caring for or working with traumatised children

Organised or ritualised abuse (OA/RA) (listed alphabetically)

+ End Ritual Abuse: http://endritualabuse.org/ is a site developed by psychologist Ellen Lacter PhD. It offers information about extreme/ritualised abuse, the production of sadistic child abuse materials, and the psychological manipulation of victims' dissociative capacities to exert long-term control. It also includes insightful articles to help survivors establish and maintain safety and work towards recovery

+ Organised Abuse: www.organisedabuse.com/info is a site developed by Scientia Associate Professor Michael Salter who has specialised in the study of organised sexual abuse, complex trauma and has researched and published widely on violence against women and children. The aim of the site is to disseminate reliable information about organised abuse to professionals, victims and survivors

+ Ritual abuse, ritual crime and healing: http://ra-info.org/about-us/ is a site that provides information and resources to survivors, their families and friends, and to professionals working therapeutically or conducting research

✦ Survivorship.org: https://survivorship.org/ is a long-standing and respected organisation that provides resources and support to survivors of extreme and severe childhood abuse. It is dedicated to improving their lives, and to equipping those who care for and work with them, through the dissemination of information, training and education, and offering a community forum for communication, validation, and peer support

✦ Working with extreme abuse. Anonymous, Miller, A., Richardson, S., Buck, S. and Ross, L., (2016). BACP: *Therapy Today*, 27, 3, pp. 14–19

✦ *Healing the Unimaginable, Treating Ritual Abuse and Mind Control,* (2012) by Alison Miller. A demanding but richly informed and essential book for experienced practitioners working with survivors of organised, and ritualised abuse

✦ *Ritual Abuse and Mind Control: The Manipulation of Attachment Needs*, (2011), edited by Orit Badouk Epstein, Joseph Schwarz and Rachel Wingfield Schwarz. Collected writings open up this subject from an attachment perspective

✦ *Shattered but Unbroken*, (2016) by Amelia van der Merwe and Valerie Sinason. Combines the narratives of survivors with contributions on causes, correlates, and interventions

Trauma and Memory

✦ Trauma and Memory: The Science and the Silenced, (2021) edited by Valerie Sinason and Ashley Conway. Elaborates the scientific and political issues around trauma memory.

✦ The Memory War: Jennifer Freyd accused her father of sexual abuse. Her parent's attempt to discredit her created a defense for countless sex offenders, by Katie Heaney. Published in *The Cut* 6/1/21: www.thecut.com/article/false-memory-syndrome-controversy.html (accessed 11/1/21)

✦ The Rise and Fall of the False Memory Syndrome Foundation, *ISSTD News*, 21/1/20. https://news.isst-d.org/the-rise-and-fall-of-the-false-memory-syndrome-foundation/ (accessed 11/1/21)

Theoretical approaches and treatment models (listed alphabetically)

Practitioners who are unfamiliar with dissociative disorders or to working with DID may prefer to start with texts that are based on their core models or familiar ways of working. Survivors can also expect to come across and be offered a variety of theoretical approaches, summarised below, although none have the monopoly on healing. It is more important that professional help is trauma-informed and based on a collaborative and companionable approach to finding what is best for each individual's journey.

Attachment-based psychotherapy:

Focuses on relationships and bonds between people. It emphasises the developing child's need to form a healthy emotional bond with at least one primary caregiver for positive social and emotional development.

- *Doing Psychotherapy: A Trauma and Attachment-Informed Approach,* (2020) by Robin Shapiro

- *Nurturing Children: From Trauma to Growth Using Attachment Theory, Psychoanalysis and Neurobiology,* (2019) by Graham Music (see description in Working with children and adolescents)

- *Trauma and the Avoidant Client: Attachment-Based Strategies for Healing, (*2010), & *Trauma and the Struggle to Open Up,* (2019) by Robert Muller

Cognitive and behavioural:

Theories and therapies elaborate the interplay between mind, thought, behaviour and action, and demonstrate how they can provoke emotions and contribute towards the maintenance of problems or towards recovery.

- *Cognitive Behavioural Approaches to the Understanding and Treatment of Dissociation,* (2013) edited by Fiona Kennedy, Helen Kennerley and David Pearson

- *DBT Skills Training Handouts and Worksheets,* 2nd edn, (2014) by Marsha Linehan

- *Reinventing Your Life* (Schema Therapy-updated 2019) by Jeffrey Young and Janet Klosko

- *The Compassionate-Mind Guide to Recovering from Trauma and PTSD: Using Compassion-Focused Therapy to Overcome Flashbacks, Shame, Guilt, and Fear,* (2013) by Deborah Lee and Sophie James

- *Trauma-Focused ACT: A Practitioner's Guide to Working with Mind, Body, and Emotion Using Acceptance and Commitment Therapy,* (2021) by Russ Harris

Creative therapies:

Use arts-based models and interventions, including music, drama, movement, art or play, with support from a trained professional. Individuals *of all ages* may find them helpful because they address issues and support expression without the need to talk or focus on the physical self.

- *A Therapeutic Treasure Box for Working with Children and Adolescents with Developmental Trauma: Creative Techniques and Activities,* (2017) by Karen Treisman

- *Trauma and Expressive Arts Therapy,* (2020) by Cathy Malchiodi

Integrative therapy:

Affirms and blends different models of therapy with consideration given to what works and why.

- *Dissociation and the Dissociative Disorders,* (2009) by Paul Dell and John O'Neil (Eds)

+ *Mindsight: Transform Your Brain with the New Science of Kindness*, (2011) by Daniel Siegel

+ *Neurobiology and Treatment of Traumatic Dissociation: Towards an Embodied Self*, (2008) by Ulrich Lanius, Sandra Paulsen and Frank Corrigan

+ *Working with Voices and Dissociative Parts – A Trauma-informed Approach*, (2019) by Dolores Mosquera (see description in Treatment books).

Internal family systems therapy:
Elaborates the relationships between parts of self or psyche and demonstrates how separation or division between parts can cause suffering.

+ *Internal Family Systems Skills Training Manual: Trauma-Informed Treatment for Anxiety, Depression, PTSD & Substance Abuse*, (2017) by Frank Anderson, Richard Schwartz and Martha Sweezy

+ *No Bad Parts: Healing Trauma and Restoring Wholeness with the Internal Family Systems Model*, (2021) by Richard Schwarz

Mindfulness:
A meditative practice that reconnects individuals to the present moment; purposefully drawing attention and focus to moment-by-moment, internal and/or external awareness.

+ *Dissociation, Mindfulness, and Creative Meditations: Trauma-Informed Practices to Facilitate Growth*, (2017) by Christine Forner

+ *Trauma-Sensitive Mindfulness: Practices for Safe and Transformative Healing*, (2018) by David Treleaven and Willoughby Britton

Polyvagal theory:
Explains the importance and value of interpersonal neurobiology in recovery from trauma, and the effect of trauma on the body and the brain.

+ *The Polyvagal Theory: Neurophysiological Foundations of Emotions, Attachment, Communication, and Self-Regulation*, (2011) by Stephen Porges

+ *The Polyvagal Theory in Therapy*, (2018) by Deb Dana

Psychoanalytic:
Theories and therapies that aim to treat mental disorders and distress by investigating the interaction of conscious and unconscious mind.

⬇ *The Dissociative Mind in Psychoanalysis: Understanding and Working with Trauma*, (2016) by Elizabeth Howell and Sheldon Itzkowitz

⬇ *Trauma, Dissociation and Multiplicity: Working on Identity and Selves*, (2010) edited by Valerie Sinason

Psychodynamic:

Based on the theories and principles of psychoanalysis, but with an increased emphasis on an individual's relationship with their external world; seeks to understand conscious and unconscious processes that influence emotions, thoughts and behaviour patterns.

⬇ *Easy Ego State Interventions: Strategies for Working with Parts*, (2016) by Robin Shapiro

Somatic (body-oriented) approaches:

Recognise that trauma and its effects are stored within the body, and cause dysregulation and restriction to movement and/or emotion.

EMDR: Eye movement, desensitisation and reprocessing:

A psychotherapeutic approach that uses visual, auditory or tactile stimuli bilaterally, (from side-to-side of the body), in a rhythmical pattern, to enable reprocessing of memory and its effects. Care needs to be exercised with RAMCOA survivors, since similar techniques have been used in some survivors' abuse, and EMDR may prove triggering or breach the therapeutic relationship.

⬇ *EMDR and Dissociation: The Progressive Approach*, (2012) by Anabel Gonzalez and Dolores Mosquera

⬇ *EMDR Toolbox: Theory and Treatment of Complex PTSD and Dissociation*, 2nd edn, (2018) by James Knipe

Sensorimotor psychotherapy:

An evolving "body-oriented talking therapy', this helps individuals stabilise, discharge and resolve physiological symptoms of trauma and adverse experiences.

⬇ *Sensorimotor Psychotherapy: Interventions for Trauma and Attachment*, (2015) by Pat Ogden and Janina Fisher

⬇ *Trauma and the Body,* (2006) by Pat Ogden, Kekuni Minton and Clare Pain

Additionally: *The Body Remembers* Volume 2, (2017) and *Eight Keys to Safe Trauma Recovery*, (2010) both by Babette Rothschild

Somatic experiencing:

Focuses on the body and perceived body sensations, to express and relieve mental and physical traumatic stress-related conditions.

⬇ *In an Unspoken Voice*, (2010) by Peter Levine

⬇ *Waking the Tiger*, (1997) by Peter Levine

<<>>

Trauma, and its legacies are increasingly recognised in all parts of society worldwide. Treatment approaches and modalities are evolving and responding to a growing need for education, understanding, and trauma-informed communities. It is hoped these resources and others will offer support and encouragement to individuals navigating a path of learning, support, and wholeness.

Glossary of terms

Affect: refers to emotion and how it is experienced in the mind or body, its effect upon individuals and/or its expression

Amnesia: forgetting significant and important information about self, others, events or periods of life

ANP: apparently normal part, manages everyday life

Blended/blending: when parts are both co-present and intermingled or merged with one-another and their separate sense of self is lost; they may share memory or awareness

Containment: creating safety, limits and/or control within the mind or in the therapeutic relationship; enables individuals to approach processing with a greater sense of choice and to manage with less emotional reactivity

Co-consciousness: when parts are aware of what is happening, and/or can observe events and share memory between themselves; it can help internal communication and collaboration

Co-present: when parts are present together, and may take shared control of the body

Coming to the front: (also *stepping forward* and *coming/being out)* when parts assume control of the body, or are present in current time; also called a "switch" or "switching"

Going inside: (also *stepping back* and *going in*) when parts relinquish control of the body to another part of self; they may or may not maintain an awareness of current time and events; also called a "switch" or "switching"

Depersonalisation: feeling detached from your body or emotions

Derealisation: feeling as if the world or others around you are unreal or unfamiliar

Dissociation: feeling disconnected from your sense of identity, from thoughts, feelings, your body, your surroundings, or memories; disruption in your sense of time; splitting

Dissociative Disorders: conditions that cause disruption to perception, awareness, emotion, behaviour, memory and/or identity. They may occur in response to stress or substance use, but have a strong connection with trauma, neglect or abuse.

DID: Dissociative Identity Disorder

OSDD: Other Specified Dissociative Disorder

Encoding: the process by which memories and experiences are stored

EP: emotional part, remembers or holds traumatic memory

Everyday self: the part of self identified in the picture book as being present most often and responsible for managing every day or ongoing life

Flashbacks: traumatic events may "*replay*" as images, sensations or feelings. Overwhelming and disorienting, individuals experience them as if they are happening current time

Grounding: reconnecting awareness to present time and establishing a sense of stability or calm; sometimes referred to as "centering", being "*centred*" or "*grounded*"

Identity alteration: marked, sometimes dramatic changes, in presentation that may affect behaviour, voice, attitude, dress, language and mood

Identity confusion: feeling conflicted about who you are

Integration: occurs when information is processed, and memory or experiences are appropriately incorporated into an individual's life history; known negative effects are diminished or resolved

RAMCOA: Ritual Abuse, Mind Control, Organised Abuse. May also appear singly as "RA", "MC" and "OA"

Parts: of self or "self-states" that form as a result of traumatic experience. They may remain the same age as the individual was when their trauma took place and may have little or no awareness of the passage of time, nor of current conditions. They may continue to function in the roles they assumed during the trauma time, in order to cope.

Processing: therapeutic treatment and/or interventions that enable traumatic material and memories to change and to decrease in negative affect, to diminish the memory's reactivity to traumatic material and the threat it represents; enables trauma memory to become part of the past and creates the possibility for meaning-making and re-energising

***Switching* or a *switch*:** when parts change places and may take control of the body; subtle changes may be called a "*shift*" or "*shifting*"

Trauma time: refers to the time during which the trauma took place. Living in trauma time infers living as though still in that time, and still subject to the same risks or threats

Traumatic experience: includes events that overpower our resources or abilities to cope. They can include overt events, such as violence or aggression, or more covert experiences, including control or neglect. They include natural disasters or interpersonal experiences that make individuals feel threatened, frightened, or overwhelmed.

Triggered: when an individual is reminded of something, and a response is activated. When a trigger is positive, the response may provoke images, feelings or sensations of comfort or pleasure; when a trigger is related to trauma or something negative, the response provoked may reactivate the original responses of pain and overwhelm, with terrifying or distressing images, feelings or sensations.

Trigger: a reminder, which can include an image/sound/smell/taste/sensation, or a scene, an action, a process, a thought, a location or a recollection. When triggers are unidentified or unknown, they seemingly activate responses randomly and without warning.

Index

polyfragmentation 23

polyvagal theory 99

Post-Traumatic Stress Disorder (PTSD) 10, 29;
    complex (CPTSD) 29

processing: bottom-up 32; consolidation 17, 38;
    creative therapies 33, 98; integration 38;
    memories 36–37; top down 33–34

professional: fatigue 46; self-care 45–46;
    supervision 31, 44; support 54

psychoanalytic 99–100

psychodynamic 100

psychosis 22, 27

ritual abuse 96

recovery 9–11, 14, 15, 19, 21, 22, 27, 31, 32, 38, 41,
    50, 51, 57, 58, 84, 85, 92, 96

resistance 57

resources: books, internet, organisations 90–101

Ross, C. 25n18

safe: external 51; internal 51; people 86–87; safety 51

Salter, M. 96

screening tools: children & adolescents 95–96;
    DES-II 42; DES-Taxon 42; SDQ-20 43

self: awareness of parts 23, 81; everyday, selves 61,
    78, 79; sense of 4, 5, 21–23, 38, 68, 79; states
    20, 25n20, 71, 72

self-care 44–46

sensorimotor 100

shame 5, 11, 37, 50, 57, 59, 65, 74, 82, 91

shift see switching

Sidran Institute 94

Silberg, J. 96

Sinason, V. 97, 100

somatic: approaches 32; experiencing 101

somatoform dissociation 20, 23, 43

splitting 74–75

stabilisation 34–35; see also safe

stamina 56–58

Steele, K. 25n19, 90, 95

stepping back and going in 22

submit 82

supervision 44

support: finding professional 54; supporters 58–59

survivorship 97

switching 20, 75; shift 22; switch 22

system 22, 37

therapeutic relationship 27, 34, 37, 42, 100

therapy see treatment

Thierry, B. de 96

trauma: affects 9–10; capital T/small t 6–7; chronic/
    complex 11, 76; continued/ongoing 1, 37, 76;
    definition 4–5; effects 10; interpersonal 27,
    31–32, 86; time 21, 22, 31, 82, 83; see also
    abuse; betrayal; memory

traumatic: effects on the brain 10; experience 1, 2, 4,
    5, 10, 17, 21, 32, 50, 76, 88; see also memory

treatment: choosing a therapist 55–56; decisions
    33; measuring progress 44; phased 34

Treisman, K. 98

trigger: definition 2; triggered 2, 22, 23, 31, 53, 59,
    80, 81, 84; warning 2–3

trust 27, 35, 54, 59, 86

Van der Hart, O. 90, 95

Van der Kolk, B. 91

Waters, F.S. 96

Wieland, S. 96